ULYSSES S. GRANT

Great American Generals
ULYSSES S. GRANT

F. Norton Boothe

LONGMEADOW
P R E S S

This 1992 edition published by
Longmeadow Press
201 High Ridge Road
Stamford CT 06904

Produced by
Brompton Books Corporation
15 Sherwood Place
Greenwich CT 06830

ISBN 0-681-41596-7

Printed in Hong Kong

0 9 8 7 6 5 4 3 2 1

PICTURE CREDITS

Brompton Photo Library: 2(all three), 11, 19(top), 23(both), 31 (bottom left), 54(top), 67(bottom), 79
Anne S.K. Brown Military Collection, Brown University: 19 (bottom), 30(top), 34, 39, 40, 44, 48, 49(top), 52(bottom), 60-61(all three).
Chicago Historical Society: 27.
Historical Society of Pennsylvania: 15(bottom).
Illinois State Historical Society: 71(bottom).
Library of Congress: 4-5, 6, 12, 13, 14, 15(top), 16, 17, 18(bottom), 21(top), 25(both), 26(both), 28, 29, 32, 35(bottom), 36, 37(both), 38(both), 41(bottom), 45, 47(top), 49(bottom), 50, 51, 52(top), 53, 54(top), 56(both), 57, 63, 64-65, 67(top), 68, 70, 71(top), 73(bottom), 74, 75(both), 76-77, 78.
National Archives: 1, 7, 8-9, 18(top), 20(left), 33, 42-43, 46, 47 (bottom), 55, 58, 59(all three), 62, 72-73(top).
National Portrait Gallery, Smithsonian Institution: 10.
Richard Natkiel: 22, 30(bottom), 66(right).
Peter Newark's Western Americana: 3, 66(bottom left).
Norfolk Southern Corporation: 20-21(bottom).
Railroad Museum of Pennsylvania: 69.
U.S. Naval History Photograph: 35(top).
Virginia State Library: 24.
V M I Museum: 41(top).
Louis A. Warren Lincoln Library and Museum, Fort Wayne, IN: 31(top left).

ACKNOWLEDGMENTS
The author and publisher would like to thank the following people who helped in the preparation of this book: Don Longabucco, who designed it; Barbara Thrasher, who edited it; and Rita Longabucco, who did the picture research.

Page 1: *Landing supplies at City Point, Virginia, Grant's headquarters, 1864-65.*

Page 2: Top: *Chickamauga, battle of the "river of death," Sept. 19-20, 1863.*

Middle: *Desperate fighting near Todd's Tavern May 6, 1864, during Battle of the Wilderness in Virginia.*

Bottom: *Union Army of the Cumberland takes Lookout Mountain November 24, 1863, at Battle of Chattanooga.*

Page 3: *Grant leading the advance in the Battle of the Wilderness.*

Below: *The 26th New York Infantry Regiment on parade outside Fort Lyons, one of many armed camps defending the nation's capital.*

Contents

An Unpromising Boy

Lincoln and Grant – their names are linked indelibly by history as their lives were linked by the whims of destiny. Had it not been for Lincoln's astute assessment of Grant's fighting abilities, his steady support of him, sometimes against all odds and the opinion of both the public and his closest advisers, Grant would never have been given the opportunity to rise to a place on the roster of the world's great generals. Had it not been for Lincoln's assassination, it is unlikely that Grant would have become the country's 18th President. But the story of history, as that of an individual's life, is full of "ifs," and that Ulysses S. Grant would ever amount to anything was a big "if" at the start of the Civil War.

In the opening sentence of his *Memoirs*, written at the close of his life, Grant stated simply: "My family is American, and has been for generations, in all its branches, direct and collateral." It is an apt summary of the forebears who converged in bringing forth the first-born son of Jesse Root and Hannah Simpson Grant on April 27, 1822, in the small frontier river town of Point Pleasant, Ohio. Matthew Grant had arrived in Massachusetts on a ship from England in 1630 and settled in Connecticut. John Simpson had come to Philadelphia from the north of Ireland around 1738. In time their progeny had rolled westward, the first in that pattern of mobility that seems endemic to America.

Jesse had worked his way from an orphaned boy of 11, apprenticed to a half-brother in the tannery business, to owning his own tannery. For a time he had lived with a judge of the Ohio Supreme Court and his wife; from them he acquired a love of reading and thirst for learning, and a taste for political argument. He was grimly determined in everything he undertook, and when, at 27, he decided he was suf-

ficiently established for marriage, he set out to find a suitable wife. Hannah Simpson was the daughter of a prosperous farmer in a neighboring settlement, a quiet, self-contained young woman approaching 23, unpretending, industrious in her domestic duties, and a devout Methodist. The house to which Jesse brought his bride was one of the best in the village of Point Pleasant, a two-room frame building overlooking the Ohio River, with a huge fireplace in the living room where Hannah did the cooking and a small bedroom with a four-poster bed, where she gave birth to their son. The names "Hiram Ulysses" were chosen for him by his Simpson grandparents – it was his grandmother who came up with "Ulysses," suggested to her perhaps by a book Jesse had lent her that inspired in both of them an admiration for the Greek warrior who had defeated the Trojans by the cunning strategy of the wooden horse. It was an odd name for a community of pioneer farmers and backwoodsmen, but it was what he was always called, or "Lyss" for short.

The following year Jesse moved his tannery to Georgetown, the new county seat. That was home to Ulysses for the next 16 years until, without any initiative on his part or interest in a military life, he went off to West Point. During those years his father's business prospered. Jesse had acquired farmland outside the town, built a substantial house in town for his growing family – in all, there were six

General Grant (center, bareheaded) as head of all U.S. forces, with his officers. Sherman is at his right hand, Sheridan (short cap) pushing to the front farther along.

children – and acquired a reputation in Georgetown as a capable, industrious, opinionated, and often contentious man.

In his *Memoirs* Grant gives only a cursory review of his life in Georgetown, summing it up as "uneventful." In a sense perhaps it was, in view of his life afterward, but less so than that of most of the boys who also grew up there.

Jesse was determined that his oldest son should have the education he had been denied. Ohio had no free schools then, only subscription schools for parents willing or able to pay the small fee for a teacher. In Georgetown the school term was limited, three months a year, as was the curriculum, the standard basics of reading, writing, arithmetic. Ulysses went to school regularly from the age of four, and, though not studiously inclined, was sufficiently dutiful to do well enough, especially in arithmetic. Wanting better for his boy, Jesse sent him to an aunt in Maysville, Kentucky, for the winter of 1836-37 in a better school, and in 1838-39 to a private Presbyterian Academy in Ripley, Ohio, where he received a better education than he thought and was more studious than he claimed.

Ulysses was small for his age in height and weight, but physically strong, and fairly good-looking with his straight nose, blue eyes, and chestnut-brown hair. Like his mother he was quiet, his voice soft and gentle, and he tended to be rather withdrawn and restrained. He did not cut much of a place in the company of the boys around him. He shied away from their swearing and profanity. It was not out of piety. On the contrary, his silent, devout mother excused him from attending church because of his unpleasant reaction to hymn singing. He was tone-deaf, and sounds supposed to exalt were to his ears a jarring cacophony. Of the six Grant children, he alone was never baptized. Though he was respectful of religion, God for him was not a being to whom he looked for guidance or support.

In another way he was different from other boys, and it was his first claim to fame. That was his uncanny skill in handling horses. When barely three he would crawl about under the horses in his father's stall, between their legs with their iron-shod hooves, without a sound or jerk that might startle them. When an alarmed neighbor tried to warn his mother he was in danger, Hannah responded, "Horses seem to understand Ulysses," and calmly went back to her housework. It was rather that Ulysses understood horses. As a small boy he rode a pony with the mastery of a trained equestrian. He was little more than six when, in his father's absence, he harnessed a colt that had never worn a collar to a sled and hauled loads of brush all day until his father's return at night. His affinity for horses exceeded any interest or emotion involving the people around him. He loved riding them and he loved any tasks of which they were a part.

Ulysses hated the tannery and everything related to it – the raw bloody hides of the slaughtered animals, the stench of processing them. He had an aversion to killing animals, which extended to a horror of game-hunting. Throughout his life he could not bear to see or eat meat unless it was so well cooked that it was almost charred. Jesse became reconciled to his son's disgust with the tanning business by his willingness to undertake the arduous jobs of hauling wagonloads of wood and goods back and forth any distance, often to towns miles away, and doing all the work on the farm requiring the use of horses.

To the extent Ulysses thought of what he wanted to become, it was either a farmer or a down-the-river trader.

Ulysses S. Grant in 1865 at the time of the victory of the Federal army over the Confederates. His clear, penetrating eyes left no one uncertain that he was in command.

Jesse had other aspirations. What he wanted for his son was a college education, but he was too thrifty to pay for it. So he went about obtaining an appointment for him to the United States Military Academy at West Point, where a good education was free. Long active in politics, he wrote to a friend who had become a congressman in Washington, who happened just then to have a vacancy in the district. When told about it, Ulysses said he wouldn't go, believing he could not meet the high academic standards for getting through the entrance examinations. Still, he was a dutiful son, and if that was what his father wanted him to do, he would try his best. If he succeeded in graduating, he did not anticipate staying in the army beyond the required two years. "A military life had no charms for me," he said in his recollections.

When he entered the Academy in 1839 he was barely past his 17th birthday, weighed 117 lbs, and was 5'1" in height, just one inch over the minimum requirement. (When he was graduated four years later he had grown to 5'8", but his weight was the same.) He discovered upon registering that his name was listed as "Ulysses S. Grant." The congressman who had appointed him, knowing the boy only as Ulysses and recalling that his mother's maiden name was Simpson, inserted the S. as his middle initial. An upperclassman, seeing the initials U.S., suggested they stood for "Uncle Sam." Another upperclassman, William Tecumseh Sherman, prof-

fered "United States." But it was Sam that stuck. "A more unpromising boy never entered the Academy," Sherman said of him later. Wearing work shoes and country clothes, with his short stature, the peculiarly awkward walk of a veteran horseman and rustic diffidence, his appearance was decidedly unmilitary. But appearance was not the sort of thing to concern the young cadet from Georgetown, as it would not concern the man who became the country's first full-ranking general since George Washington. What concerned him was the possibility of failing.

He was better prepared than he thought, and passed his entrance examinations without difficulty. He was less prepared for the strict discipline and regulations of every hour of existence. At home in Georgetown he had never been re-

Among the members of Grant's staff was Frederick T. Dent (standing just left of tent pole), whose sister Julia had been married to Ulysses in 1848 after a long romance, their wedding having been postponed because of the Mexican War.

Except in mathematics, for which he had a flair, and horsemanship, of course, in which he excelled (but for which there was no academic credit), his class standings were, at best, moderate. According to his plebe-year roommate, Rufus Ingalls (who was to serve under him years later), he was "so quick in his perceptions that he usually made very fair recitations even with little preparation." In general, he found the curriculum rather uninteresting. Nevertheless, upon graduation he stood 21st in a class of 39.

Although he was considered a "good fellow" by his classmates, he made few real friends. One of them was Simon Bolivar Buckner, who would turn up in the years to come at several critical points in his career.

He had hoped to be assigned to the cavalry, or dragoons, as they were then called, after graduation. Instead, he was assigned to the Fourth Infantry as a brevet 2d lieutenant. After a summer furlough at his parents' new home in Bethel, Ohio, he reported for duty at the end of September at Jefferson Barracks, St. Louis, the largest military post in the country at that time.

For Grant it turned out to be a fortuitous location. Five miles west was White Haven, the plantation-like home of his roommate his last year at West Point, Frederick Dent. Before going off to his assignment elsewhere, Fred had urged his friend to pay his family a visit. Having his own horse he had brought from Ohio, Grant one day rode out to make the acquaintance of Colonel Dent (as he called himself) and his sizable household. Though the Colonel himself was somewhat pretentious, Grant found the family congenial, and he was invited warmly to come back as often as possible. On one of these visits he met the oldest daughter, Julia, who had just returned from boarding school in St. Louis. From that day his visits to White Haven became more frequent.

Julia was then 17, a fully formed young woman, and, while not a beauty in any conventional sense, she was wonderful company, vivacious, tactful, caring, and an excellent horsewoman. If Grant noticed a slight squint in one of her eyes, it did not detract from the pleasure of being with her, in their walks and rides, in the bouquets of flowers she gathered for him to take back to the post. He had never known that kind of caring. His mother was not given to displays of affection. Romance had been absent in the home of his parents and in the closed world of his life in Georgetown and the Academy. He might not have recognized it as soon as he did had it not been that in May 1844 he and his fellow officers were ordered to leave immediately for Louisiana because of the imminence of war with Mexico. When he realized this meant a separation from Julia Dent, he galloped out to White Haven and mustered the courage to ask her what she too was suddenly aware she wanted to hear – when he came back would she marry him? It was to be four years before the pledge they exchanged that day could be fulfilled, but neither ever wavered from the certainty that they would spend their lives together. As they did, totally committed to one another whatever befell them.

quired to fold his clothes and put them away or keep his shoes shined, and his parents had never scolded or punished him. The rules at West Point and the reprimands he received did little to change his habits. After four years the sum of the demerits chalked up against him were all for untidiness and inattention, none for disobedience or resentment.

The Mexican War and Peacetime Trials

The direct cause of the Mexican War was the annexation of Texas by the U.S. Congress in 1845, ignited by the rhetoric about Manifest Destiny during the 1844 campaign that elected James K. Polk as President. The Mexicans insisted that the southern boundary of Texas was the Neuces River, not the Rio Grande as the Texans claimed. The Neuces emptied into the Gulf of Mexico at the small adobe village of Corpus Christi. One hundred fifty miles to the south the Rio Grande emptied into the Gulf of Matamoros. The area between the two rivers was unpopulated and virtually uncharted. Zachary Taylor, with a 3000-man army, was ordered into the disputed territory to do what he could to provoke the Mexicans into an act of war. That was achieved by hastily building a fort opposite Matamoros 25 miles from Port Isabel on the north bank of the Rio Grande, where the main body halted to take supplies from ships. The Mexicans promptly shelled the fort, killing its commandant, Maj. Jacob Brown (for whom Brownsville, Texas, is named). Congress declared war. The President called for volunteers.

In his *Memoirs* Grant states: "I do not think there was ever a more wicked war than that waged by the United States on Mexico . . . it was on our part most unjust." Despite his strong opinions on the subject, he considered his "supreme duty was to my flag." He crossed the Rio Grande with the Army of Occupation, as the expeditionary force was called, and became engaged in a war that was to be the proving ground for many of the country's best military leaders who were to figure prominently in the much greater conflict for the dominion of that flag on American soil.

Now a full 2nd lieutenant, Grant was assigned to duty as quartermaster of his regiment, conducting the wagon train, packing up and moving tents and blankets, pots and pans, issuing supplies, in effect, the regimental drudgework. His place was at the rear of the army away from the scene of battle and military renown. He did not remain at the rear long. When the army reached Monterrey, after marching 200 miles from Matamoros, he turned over the command to a subordinate and rode helter-skelter through bullet-swept streets to bring up a supply of ammunition. Before the war was over he seized other opportunities, displaying ingenuity and spectacular bravery. He was reassigned to Gen. Winfield Scott's command, which landed at Vera Cruz and took the city, and he participated in the long march of Scott's forces to Mexico City over treacherous mountains. Present at the battle of Cerro Gordo, a mountain pass about 50 miles from Vera Cruz, he was enthusiastic about the officer whose engineering skill made it a victory – Robert E. Lee. As one of the line officers in the first wave against Cha-

Below: *During the Mexican War Grant served under Zachary Taylor (center, bareheaded), whose "rough and ready" style as a field general and informal manner in camp he adopted as his own.*

Opposite: *The storming of Chapultepec in September 1847 gave Grant an opportunity to display initiative and daring in instigating and carrying out a bold attack.*

pultepec, an outlying suburb of Mexico City, Grant initiated a spontaneous act of derring-do that won him promotion to captain.

Far more important than his promotion and exploits in a war of which he disapproved was what he learned about the command personalities of the generals under whom he served, as well as about the individual qualities of the officers he served with. That insight would be invaluable to him later in selecting the men he would command and in sizing up his foe.

It has often been said that in "Old Rough and Ready" Zachary Taylor he found the style of field general he would become, caring not a fig for military finery or decorum, sauntering around army posts in blue jeans and ordinary soldiers' boots, inclined to do the best he could with the means given him without troubling the administration with demands, facing danger in the field along with his men, accepting responsibility calmly. Their respect for one another was mutual. On one occasion, seeing Grant up to his waist in water working with his men to clear underwater obstructions, Taylor said, "I wish I had more officers like Grant, who would stand ready to set a personal example when needed."

Winfield Scott, the country's top-ranking general, was the complete opposite. A tall, grandiose man, majestic at all times, he always wore his full uniform with all the decorations allowed by law, often speaking of himself in the third person, never without the accompaniment of his staff. A supreme strategist rather than battlefield leader, he was successful in organizing and carrying through bold and risky maneuvers, such as his long march to Mexico City cut off from his supply lines and vastly outnumbered. Grant's admiration for him was close to awe. Little did he suspect on that march that he would one day command maneuvers

as bold and risky, let alone that he would hold a rank even higher than that of Scott.

During the eight months Grant spent in Mexico City he came to love the country. He enjoyed riding out to view mountains and valleys and lakes, usually alone, sometimes with his friend from West Point, Simon Bolivar Buckner. Buckner said, "The Mexican War was our romance." But the real romance Ulysses Grant held close, even in the faraway beauty of Mexico, was waiting for him in St. Louis.

He and Julia were married there on August 22, 1848, in Colonel Dent's townhouse. It was a fashionable wedding, for the Dents were a family of considerable social standing. Among the groom's attendants was a friend from West Point, James "Pete" Longstreet, a gentle-mannered South Carolinian, also just back from the Mexican War. They were to share in a number of future events, but not in the same aisle.

Having served the two years, and more, of service required of a graduate of West Point, Grant could have resigned his commission to enter a better paying profession. His prestige as a veteran of a successful war was a good recommendation. But he did not want to go into his father's business, was not sufficiently eager about any other, and so he elected to remain in the peacetime army, despite its low pay and lack of opportunity for advancement. He and Julia spent the next three and a half years at barracks in Sackets Harbor on Lake Ontario, New York, and at Fort Wayne in Detroit. Their first son, named Frederick Dent after the Colonel, was born, and they were as happy together as they had known they would be. Then, in the spring of 1852, Grant was transferred to the West Coast. The journey by way of the Isthmus of Panama was long and arduous, Julia was expecting the birth of a second child in July, and it was decided that Ulysses would go ahead and his family join him

as soon as he had established suitable living conditions for them. It was as well that Julia did not accompany him on that journey. The ship that sailed from New York for that distant post encountered serious obstacles, including an epidemic of cholera that took the lives of more than 100 of the men aboard and over 40 of their wives and children. It would be two years before he would be reunited with Julia. Those years were a dismal chapter in the life of Ulysses S. Grant.

It was clear to him that his army pay was insufficient to maintain a family under the conditions prevailing on the West Coast. Repeated efforts to augment it by outside activities, as the other men did, failed miserably, doomed by bad luck and his naiveté in business ventures. The posts to which he was assigned, first Fort Vancouver on the Columbia River, then Humboldt Bay 240 miles north of San Francisco, were remote and dreary, providing little to occupy his time or attention. Letters from Julia were long delayed in reaching him. He had no interest in the diversions of his fellow officers – dancing, billiards, hunting, women. Grant began drinking, but he could not handle alcohol. It did not make him more sociable or obstreperous, it simply alienated him from the world around him and its duties. Those who knew and liked him were understanding. His strict superior officer, Col. Robert Buchanan, who did not like him, was not. When one day Grant, acting as paymaster, was unfit to count money, Buchanan demanded he should resign or stand trial. Grant resigned. No reason for his resignation was recorded in its official acceptance by the Secretary of War. It seems likely that he would easily have survived a trial, even more likely that he had already given up on an army career, a profession he had not chosen and never particularly liked. By an irony of fate, had he remained in the army, he would undoubtedly have been kept patrolling the Far West, as other trained officers whom the government kept at their posts during the Civil War. It was because he was out of the army but a West Pointer that his chance came when volunteer forces had to be drilled and trained.

But none of that was on the horizon when he came home, empty-handed, at the end of the summer of 1854. Such was the state of his fortunes that army friends in San Francisco raised the money for his passage to New York. Once there, completely penniless, he had to borrow money from Simon Bolivar Buckner to get back to St. Louis. His return, if under a shadow, was for him the comfort he had been longing for. At last he was able to see his second son, now two years old, named after his father, but always called "Buck." He would never again be separated for long from his wife and children.

Julia's father had given her as a wedding present some acreage of uncleared, untilled land outside of St. Louis. His son-in-law now commenced his struggle to support his family by turning that land into a farm. From the trees he felled he built a sturdy, two-story house he called "Hardscrabble." To tide over until the farm should become self-

sustaining, he would cut and load firewood on to a wagon, haul it into St. Louis to sell on street corners at $4 a cord. His responsibilities grew – a daughter Nellie and his last son Jesse came along to complete the family.

Despite long hard hours of back-breaking labor, the farm never became self-sustaining. A failed wheat crop one year and the severe depression of 1857 that proved disastrous to farmers forced him to sell his stock, crops, and farm implements and seek other employment. A partnership with a cousin of Julia's who was in real estate in St. Louis lasted less than a year. There was nothing left for him but the humiliation of appealing to his father, who gave him a place in a leather and harness store he owned in Galena, Illinois, run by two of his other sons, Orvil and Simpson.

Galena was then the largest river port north of St. Louis, an important center of commerce with a population of 12,000. In the summer of 1860 it became the home town that would proudly claim Grant as its own when he was hailed as the country's hero and then its president. At the time, however, its solid townsmen were little impressed by the silent bearded man in a battered army hat and fading blue army overcoat who appeared to be no more than a sort of back-office clerk in the Grant leather store. No one would have suspected the boisterous joy with which his children greeted his return home each evening, or his fun in romping and tumbling about with them on the floor. Or the unwavering faith Julia had that "we will not always be in this condition." Her optimistic nature and confidence in him, whatever his immediate circumstances, were ever sustaining. Nor could anyone have suspected that summer of 1860 that in just 11 months an event would occur that would definitively change their lives, the life of the country, and, in particular, that of Capt. Sam Grant.

Left: *General Winfield Scott, who commanded the long, arduous march to Mexico City, was a supreme strategist and majestic figure.*

Right: *An idealized representation of Grant at the capture of Mexico City.*

Secession and Civil War

In November 1860 Abraham Lincoln of Springfield, Ill., was elected President. In December South Carolina seceded from the Union and in the first two months of 1861 formed with six other states the Confederate States of America, electing as President Jefferson Davis, a graduate of West Point and veteran of the Mexican War who had served as Secretary of War in Franklin Pierce's administration and as a Senator from Mississippi. In April Confederate artillery under Gen. Pierre Gustave Toutant Beauregard fired on Fort Sumter in Charleston Harbor, forcing its commanding officer, Maj. Robert Anderson, to surrender and haul down the U.S. flag. On April 15 the President called for 75,000 volunteers to put down the insurrection. The next evening the men of Galena packed its courthouse to hear speeches from, among others, the district's congressman, Elihu B. Washburne, and one of the town's leading young lawyers, John A. Rawlins. In the course of a fiery 45-minute speech Rawlins cried: "We will stand by the flag of our country." Walking home with his brother Orvil afterward, Grant said quietly, "I think I ought to go into the service."

Up to then he had been little interested in political matters. His father Jesse was rabidly opposed to slavery and in principle his son agreed with him. Colonel Dent, on the other hand, was a slave-owner and proud of it. He had given Julia her personal slave when she was 17, and slaves later given her by her father were part of their household when they were on the farm. But Rawlins's words had struck a conviction rooted deep in Ulysses S. Grant. The issue for him was not so much the institution of slavery, deplorable as it was, but loyalty to the Union. Legitimate disagreement, even opposition, was one thing; it could be resolved. Secession was another; it was treason.

In the succeeding days he was active enlisting men for a Galena company of volunteers and went off with them to a camp in Springfield to drill them. He declined the captaincy of the company. As a West Point graduate and an officer with professional army service he considered that to take command of a volunteer company would be a demotion. He expected at the very least a commission as colonel and a regiment of his own to command. It was not to be easy to realize.

He met with rebuffs wherever he turned, and his application to the Secretary of War in Washington went unanswered. Since boyhood he had had an obdurate quality about him; once he set out on a certain road he would continue on it whether or not he knew exactly where it led. In the first months of the war he was sorely tested, but he persisted. Finally the governor of the state, Richard Yates, appointed him colonel at the head of the Twenty-first Illinois Regiment. It was a regiment of unruly volunteers,

THE UNION MUST AND SHALL BE PRESERVED

FREE SPEECH.
FREE HOMES.
FREE TERRITORY.

PROTECTION TO AMERICAN INDUSTRY

FOR PRESIDENT
ABRAHAM LINCOLN
OF ILLINOIS

FOR VICE PRESIDENT
HANNIBAL HAMLIN
OF MAINE

Left: *A political poster of the Republican Party in the 1860 Presidential campaign asserting Lincoln's conviction that "The Union must be preserved."*

Above: *The attack on Fort Sumter in Charleston Harbor, S.C., on April 13, 1861, was the decisive act of the newly formed secessionist Confederate States of America precipitating the outbreak of war between North and South.*

Right: *Lincoln's immediate call for 75,000 militia to quell insurrection in South Carolina brought instant enlistment of Yankee volunteers enthusiastic about "marching into Dixie."*

An artist's sketch showing President Lincoln and Winfield Scott, general in chief of the U.S. Army, reviewing the first regiments of three-year enlistees parading up Pennsylvania Avenue past the White House.

but he had his commission and his own command. Furthermore, he had those volunteers firmly under his control from the moment he took over at Camp Yates.

He was stationed in Mexico, Missouri, when toward the end of July Lincoln, faced with a growing army, had to submit the names of 26 men to Congress for promotion to brigadier general. Congressman Washburne, who had sponsored his fellow townsman for a colonelcy, now endorsed him for one of these promotions. Grant learned in early August from the papers that he was among those named. His first move was to ask John A. Rawlins to join his staff. Throughout the war and later the two men were knit by an intense friendship, indispensable to Grant. For in addition to his clear-headedness when confronted with conflicting propositions, Rawlins was an avid teetotaler. His father had died an alcoholic, and he hated the "demon rum." He did not hesitate to admonish Grant about the danger of drinking or read him the riot act on the very few occasions (never detrimental to the outcome of a battle) when his warnings were not heeded.

At that time the overall command in the West had passed to a nationally known figure, Maj. Gen. John Charles Frémont. Frémont was a volatile, rather romantic man who had made a glamorous reputation for a series of expeditions that mapped the Oregon Trail and the California Trail. In 1856 he had been the first presidential nominee of the Republican Party. He owed the new command partly to the intervention of Congressman Frank Blair, Jr., of St. Louis, organizer of Missouri's Unionists. Frémont started well, announcing an ambitious plan for raising a huge army and moving down the Mississippi escorted by a fleet of gunboats, but he was better at making grandiose plans than carrying them out. His dictatorial conduct, serious bungling, and defiance of Lincoln's policy caused Winfield Scott, then general-in-chief in Washington, to dismiss him from his command. Before he disappeared from the scene, he performed an important service for the army in the West.

He needed a man to command the troops assembling in Cairo, Illinois, for future offensives to the South. The last officer he interviewed was the scruffy new brigadier general at the head of the Twenty-first Illinois Regiment. Impressed by Grant's dogged persistence and iron will, Frémont gave him command of the military headquarters at Cairo. And that is where Grant the general began to emerge.

Unlike most of his colleagues, Grant grasped the importance to Lincoln of holding Kentucky in the Union. Knowing Confederate forces were invading the state in large numbers, he quickly occupied the town of Paducah, Kentucky, at the mouth of the Tennessee River invasion route. In November 1861 he converted a "demonstration" against the tiny town of Belmont into an attack. His object was to seize Columbus, Kentucky, across the river before Confederate forces, headed by Gen. Leonidas Polk, did. The action at Belmont turned out to be a pointless battle for both sides, but it did buck up Federal morale and mark a distinctive quality about Grant. In a period when generals felt unready to meet the enemy and Lincoln was growing desperate for action, Grant showed himself willing to fight.

After Frémont's departure the command in the West was divided between Gen. Henry W. Halleck, Department of Missouri (stretching from Arkansas and western Kentucky to Minnesota and Wisconsin) and Brig. Gen. Don Carlos Buell, who replaced William T. Sherman as commander of the Department of Ohio (Kentucky east of the Cumberland and Tennessee rivers) when Sherman had a nervous breakdown and was temporarily out of action. Halleck had been a member of the engineering faculty when Grant entered West Point. He resigned from the army in 1854 to go to California, where he had a highly successful career in business until re-entering the army in 1861 at the start of the war. Halleck was brilliant – his nickname was "Old Brains" – and respected as a military theoretician. But he offended many with his arrogant and self-seeking manner. His goal was to expand his command and make sure no blame of any sort fell to him. An excellent administrator and skillful manager of the army's relations with politicians and press, he was seen as the pre-eminent scholar of warfare in the country.

But Halleck and Buell did not act in concert, as Lincoln expected, each preferring to continue building, arming, and training his separate forces. Halleck thought that the original idea of advancing down the Mississippi was impractical because of the 140 guns Polk had dug into the bluffs at Columbus. He was more drawn to avenues of invasion provided by the Cumberland and Tennessee rivers.

The Federal gunboat fleet had been converted into ironclad boats that could hold up against heavy guns like those at Columbus or Fort Henry, a Confederate stronghold on the Tennessee River. Seven of them were under Andrew Hull Foote, designated a flag officer, equivalent to a general at a time when the navy was not yet using the grade of admiral. The gunboats were based at Grant's headquarters in Cairo. Foote and Grant agreed to work together in an expedition up the Tennessee for a move on Fort Henry.

On February 2, 1862, Grant loaded 17,000 men on steamboats and started up the Tennessee with Foote's gunboats. The river was coming up swiftly, and by the morning of February 5 the water was two feet deep at the base of the flagpole on Fort Henry. Several of the fort's guns were soon under water, and rapid firing from the gunboats quickly disabled the two most important ones. Fort Henry held out for two hours, then the flag went down with the gunboats within 200 yards. Its commander, Col. Lloyd Tilghman, went to the *Cincinnati* and surrendered formally to Foote. That afternoon Grant wired Halleck "Fort Henry is ours." Albert Sidney Johnston's Tennessee line had been breached, the war in the West was starting to move.

The day after Fort Henry fell Albert D. Richardson of the *New York Tribune* went to see Grant to say goodbye before going off to report his story. "You'd better wait a day or two," Grant said. "I'm going over to attack Fort Donelson tomorrow." He knew he could not hold his prize, Fort Henry, if he did not take Donelson. Twelve miles away on the Cumberland River Fort Donelson was being reinforced by the 2500 men retreating overland from Fort Henry. Inexplicably, General Johnston, aware that he was being seriously threatened, left the 5000 men already there at Fort Donelson and gradually committed 12,000 more. He then made the mistake of leaving in command a trio of brigadier generals – Gideon J. Pillow (the only Confederate commander whom Grant held in open contempt), John B. Lloyd, and Simon Bolivar Buckner. Pillow was the highest in authority.

On February 12 Grant marched his 15,000 men to invest Fort Donelson, summoning Brig. Gen. Lew Wallace, left at Fort Henry, to join him with his 2000 men. Next morning Foote's gunboat flotilla and 12 army transports with 10,000 troops arrived and tied up three miles from Donelson. Foote's first attack from the river on February 14 was repulsed, Foote was injured and had to retire. Next day Grant held a conference aboard his headquarters ship *Tigress* with Foote and the three generals under his command – Lew Wallace, Charles F. Smith, and John A. McClernand, an Illinois politician who had obtained an appointment as brigadier general and treated the proceeding as though he were at a political caucus. Grant had no intention of delaying action in wordy discussion about it. He cut the conference short quickly and gave the order that all were to be ready to leave at a moment's notice.

They took up positions west, center and east of the fort, in the path of the forces trying to fight their way out of the fort and on to the road eastward to Confederate-held Nashville. In the freezing dawn of February 15, while Grant was with the wounded Foote aboard the flagship, the Confederates attacked heavily and by 9AM had driven back and broken the Union right and most of the center, opening the road to their escape. McClernand's troops were driven off by the Confederate cavalry officer, Nathan Bedford Forrest, and his expert horsemen. Informed of the situation, Grant galloped along the line and decided, with the bold decisiveness he would show often in a crisis, to attack with his left. His order to Gen. Smith to assault at once was executed flawlessly. By nightfall his troops had possession of the entire outer line of Confederate trenches. Both Pillow and Lloyd refused to surrender, yielded their commands to Buckner, and managed to escape on the river. Forrest and his cavalry succeeded in crossing an icy breakwater before dawn on February 16 and got to Nashville in just two days.

Buckner sent a messenger to Grant under a white flag with an offer to discuss surrender terms, hoping that his old

Henry W. Halleck, a brilliant military theoretician, given command of the Department of Missouri in March 1862, was better at administrative detail than in relations with his officers.

Above: *Brigadier General Don Carlos Buell replaced Sherman as commander of the Department of Ohio in June 1862.*

Below: *Lew Wallace, who fought under Grant at Donelson and Shiloh, gained success after the war for his novel* Ben Hur.

friend would be lenient. Grant's reply was: "No terms except unconditional and immediate surrender can be accepted." Buckner had no choice but to accept the harsh terms. After the surrender Grant was surprised to find Lew Wallace cheerfully having breakfast with Buckner at an inn in the town of Dover outside the fort. Buckner was apprehensive about whether, as a captured West Point man, he would be treated as a traitor rather than a prisoner of war. Grant assured him he would be sent with the men north as a prisoner of war to be exchanged later. And he repaid the favor done him in New York eight years earlier by offering Buckner the use of his purse during the time of his captivity. (Buckner was exchanged six months later, in August, and fought in a number of subsequent battles.)

This victory, the first real Federal victory of the war, touched off celebrations all across the North. The general responsible for it was hailed as "Unconditional Surrender" Grant. Halleck offered him no congratulations. Instead, he telegraphed Washington: "Make Buell, Grant and Pope major generals and give me command in the West. I ask this in return for Forts Henry and Donelson." (John Pope was then serving under Halleck in the Department of Missouri. Neither he nor Buell had any part in the victory). Lincoln replied by promoting Grant to major general and ignoring Halleck's other recommendations. That made Grant second only to Halleck in the Western theater.

An interesting side effect of Grant's sudden acclaim was that the admiring public, reading in the papers that he was smoking a cigar in the midst of the conflict, began deluging him with boxes of the best cigars. Until then he had been only a light smoker. With such a supply on hand, far exceeding what he could give away, he took to smoking more and more until he was rarely seen without a cigar in his mouth. One aide said he went through about 20 cigars a day.

Grant saw Donelson not as a crowning victory, but as the important second action in a series that would secure the state of Tennessee for the Union. He moved promptly through Tennessee, arriving in Nashville before Buell, who, heading there at a slower pace, could do no more than join in the invasion already launched. The Confederates had already received word from Gen. Johnston, after the surrender of Fort Donelson, to prepare to abandon the city.

It was galling to Halleck that his subordinate was showing such independence. He wired Grant that he had placed Gen. Smith in command of the expedition up the Tennessee and rebuked him for going to Nashville. Disheartened, Grant set about attending to the details of transfer. Then a second stinging rebuke arrived from Halleck accusing him of neglecting often-repeated orders to report the strength of his command. To Washington he complained not only of having had no communication from Grant but of having heard that he had "resumed his former bad habits," and saying that he should be placed under arrest for insubordination. In the end Lincoln himself called a halt to the attempt to smear Grant. He gave Halleck, at last, what he had been wanting, overall command of forces in the West. He evidently also set him straight about the ruckus over Grant. At any rate, when Halleck received word from Grant that he was yielding his command as ordered so that the offensive could go forward, he replied: "You cannot be relieved from your command. . . . I wish you, as soon as your army is in the field, to assume the immediate command and lead it on to new victories."

Left: *After the surrender of Fort Henry in February 1862 Grant led his 15,000 men 12 miles overland for an assault on Fort Donelson, the first real Federal victory of the war.*

Below: *Confederate General Simon Bolivar Buckner, who had befriended Grant in prior days, was taken captive with his 17,000 men at Donelson under the famous terms of "Unconditional Surrender."*

Bloody Shiloh

Meanwhile, Confederate forces in the West, under the command of one of the South's finest generals, Albert Sidney Johnston, set out to repair the damage to their position caused by the fall of Forts Henry and Donelson. Johnston had as his second-in-command the illustrious Gen. P. G. T. Beauregard, who had been transferred from the East. Together they assembled an army of some 40,000 men at Corinth, Mississippi, consisting of units under Generals Braxton Bragg, William J. Hardee, James C. Breckinridge, and Leonidas Polk (a West Pointer who had become a bishop in the Episcopal Church until the outbreak of the war brought him to less priestly service to his native Southland). The plan was to launch an offensive attack in the vicinity of Pittsburg Landing, the point on the Tennessee River 22 miles to the north where Grant had ordered the concentration of his forces upon retaking command.

Grant was unaware of the size of the Confederate force at Corinth and not far from his own camps, which extended along the west side of the Tennessee and south toward the small meetinghouse called Shiloh Church. He had 33,000 troops in six divisions – those of John A. McClernand, William H. Wallace, Lew Wallace, Steven A. Hurlbut, William Tecumseh Sherman, and Benjamin M. Prentiss. The forces of Gen. Don Carlos Buell's Army of the Ohio were moving southeast from Nashville to join them. It was Grant's plan to move in one fell swoop upon Corinth, on the assumption that his forces greatly outnumbered the Confederates, who, he was confident, would not venture out of the good defensive position at Corinth. No trenches were dug, no fortifications built. Primary attention was concentrated on drilling the soldiers, in sore need of it, for many of them were volunteers and did not yet know how to load a rifle.

Grant was especially glad to have Sherman along. William Tecumseh Sherman was a tall thin man with piercing eyes, sunken temples and sandy red hair and beard – brilliant, eccentric, often uncertain, intensely highstrung. His first battle experience at First Manassas, which ended in the panicked rout of Union forces, and his erratic behavior when he was afterward a command officer at Louisville had led to some sort of mental collapse. But he had returned to the field as division commander and co-operated readily in a subordinate position during Grant's campaign against the river forts. It was then that they formed their lifelong friendship and potent military partnership. The two now concurred in their confidence that the Confederates were staying put in Corinth.

On the afternoon of April 5, 1862, Grant wrote Halleck: "I scarcely have the faintest idea of an attack . . . being made

on us, but will be prepared should such a thing take place."
That same afternoon men from Sherman's outfit came back
from investigating saying they had been fired on. Sherman
laughed it off as no more than roving skirmishers; every day
there was a little of that going on round and about. Asleep in
their tents that night the men did not notice the clamorous
noise a little to the south of them. It was Confederate
soldiers, vast numbers of them, who had marched through
mud and rain from Corinth and were less than two miles
away waiting for dawn when they could strike.

At 3 AM Sunday, April 6, heavy firing on a brigade of Prentiss's division on patrol a half mile from camp on the edge of
a farm field alerted the men that something serious was
afoot. By the time Col. Everett Peabody, the brigade's commander, could get word to Prentiss and reinforcements
sent up the whole Confederate line was advancing, thousands upon thousands, amid volleys of gunfire. When the
sound of heavy firing from the first collision at 5 AM reached
Johnston's temporary headquarters on the Pittsburg-
Corinth road, Beauregard was for abandoning the battle.
But Johnston said, "The battle has opened, it's too late to
back out now," and, riding forward, added, "Tonight we will
water our horses in the Tennessee River." The full impact of
the initial Confederate assault slashed into Sherman's division. The men, still groggy from sleep, were standing over
their campfires cooking breakfast. Still clad in little but their
blankets they made a run for it, leaving their cooking pots to
their hungry, and gleeful, attackers. Johnston rode through
one of the captured camps and found some of his men loot-

Above: *An erratic man with a highstrung temperament and piercing eyes, William Tecumseh Sherman showed both mastery and ferocity as a general and proved steadfast and loyal as a friend to Grant.*

Far left: *One of the Confederacy's most respected generals, Albert Sidney Johnston was mortally wounded during the first day of the fighting at Shiloh, at the moment victory seemed assured.*

Left: *The Memphis and Charleston Railway station at Corinth, Mississippi, which supplied the Confederate army. After the Union victory at Shiloh it was abandoned to advancing Federal troops.*

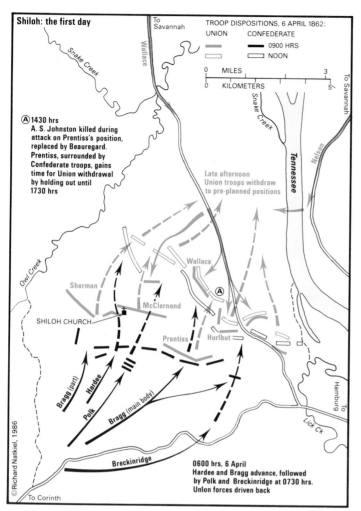

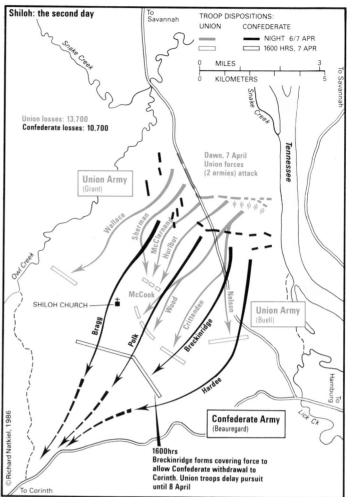

Maps showing the positions of Confederate and Union armies in the treacherous grounds around Shiloh Church on April 6 and 7, 1862. Though heavy reinforcements during the night turned defeat into a Federal victory, casualties were staggering.

ing. When one proudly showed him a fine brier pipe he had taken from a Yankee colonel's hut, Johnston rebuked him, then, seeing he had hurt the subaltern's feelings by his harsh tone, leaned down from his horse to pick up a tin cup from the table and said, "Let this be my share of the spoils today." He used it thereafter instead of a sword to direct the battle. It was still grasped in his hand that afternoon when he was mortally wounded.

Grant's breakfast was also cut short. At the Savannah headquarters 12 miles downriver he heard the roar of guns as Prentiss's whole division fell under fire at 6 AM. Ordering that Buell summon his men immediately (some spread back as far as Nashville), he started for Pittsburg Landing on a frustratingly slow river boat, pausing at Crump's Landing only long enough to call across the water to Gen. Lew Wallace to get his men ready to move. Reaching Pittsburg Landing about 9 AM, Grant, limping from a sprained ankle, was helped on to his horse and with a crutch strapped to his saddle headed up the high bluff to establish a line to stop the frightened men running away. In mid-afternoon he joined Sherman, who had been in the saddle from the first shot. In the course of that whole dreadful Sunday trying to shore up the battered armies, Sherman had two horses shot from under him and his hand wounded.

The fields and woods between Shiloh meetinghouse and the river were bounded to the south and north by marshy creeks. Johnston's aim was to drive Grant's men not to the river, across which they might escape, but northward to Owl and Snake Creeks, where they might be trapped and cut down. Beauregard was sent to the left and took Shiloh church. Hardee's men, to his right, began the relentless slaughter of Prentiss's men.

The Union army was now fighting in a three-sided box – the right flank on swampy Owl Creek, which ran into Snake Creek (which in turn ran into the Tennessee River) and the left flank on Lick Creek, also running to the river in the Union army's rear. It was through the only entrance to this box that the Confederates poured in an avalanche, their idea to cut off any possibility of escape or rescue by boat. The bulk of their forces, which should have been near Lick Creek, were lined up in parallel lines: Hardee, Bragg, and Polk's corps in the rear. No single commander was responsible for any particular part of the line, and in such a densely wooded area with winding ravines and country roads, control of the troops was difficult.

Grant arrived on the field to find all five of his divisions in a desperate struggle for survival. He moved from point to point within the lines to encourage commanders and men and to know firsthand what was happening. Everywhere the Confederates were pushing forward, and the Union situation looked hopeless. But in the center of the line was a naturally strong defensive position, a dense wood with open fields on either side. Here Prentiss rallied some of his fleeing men. Eleven times the Confederates charged the new line, to be driven back each time by fire so stinging and unremitting that the Confederates called it "The Hornet's Nest" – the name by which it is called to this day. On the flanks, however, Sherman and McClernand were slowly forced back on the right, and at the opposite end of the field the Union line was enveloped. Here the Confederate general, Albert Sidney Johnston, bled to death from a severed artery in his thigh; he had sent away his staff surgeon, riding beside him, to care for some wounded Union soldiers. Between that spot, now Johnston's Monument, to the south, and the Hornet's Nest, a short distance north of it, is a location remembered as Bloody Pond because its waters were stained red by the blood of wounded men from both sides who dragged themselves to it.

The Confederates never did break the Hornet's Nest. Hardee's men finally succeeded in surrounding it. Prentiss's men could hold out no longer and surrendered, a serious loss of some 2200, magnified by the deaths of Col. Peabody and Gen. W. H. L. Wallace. Near the river a number of Union guns were hastily put into position to protect Pittsburg

Landing. In a final desperate effort, two brigades of Confederates charged into the fire of massed artillery. But Gen. Buell had arrived by gunboat, and a vanguard of his forces helped defeat this effort. But April 6 was a Confederate victory, celebrated as such in the camps the Rebels had captured from the enemy.

The night of April 6-7 was dismal, rainy, and grim. Grant wandered about, seeking somewhere to rest his swollen leg. The loghouse near the landing was being used as a hospital. He tried it for a while, but he could never stand the sight of blood, and there was plenty of it, along with the grating sound of surgeons' saws hacking away at the arms and legs of the wounded. He ended by sitting in the wet and cold under a tree, planning his attack for the next day. He was not going to turn back; he was too obdurate to retreat. During the night Sherman found him. "We've had a devil of a day, haven't we?" he said to his friend. Grant replied, "Yes – lick 'em tomorrow though."

His original forces of about 33,000 men had been drastically reduced. But during the evening and night Buell's men, totaling 25,000, were transported division by division across the Tennessee, all fresh and well trained. Lew Wallace too finally arrived with his 5000 men – he had taken the

Left: *The initial Confederate assault at Shiloh caught Union soldiers offguard, cooking breakfast over campfires. Riding through the quickly abandoned camps, General Johnston exchanged the sword he is seen brandishing here for a tin cup and used it to direct the battle. It was still in his hand when he died that afternoon.*

Left: *When Grant reached Pittsburg Landing the morning of April 6 he found Union forces cowering under the bluffs of the Tennesee River. Mounting the bluff on horseback, he established a line and rallied his frightened men from a post on the high ground at right.*

wrong road from Crump's Landing and did not make it to the battlefield until after dark.

Beauregard, in command since Johnston's death, made no effort to hold together his scattered troops. He was expecting reinforcements from Gen. Earl Van Dorn, moving up from Arkansas, not knowing that Van Dorn had been halted by the swollen Mississippi. So confident was he that he had Grant where he wanted him and could easily finish him off in the morning that he wired Jefferson Davis in Richmond "Complete Victory." Most Confederate soldiers were sure the Federals would flee across the river in the dark rather than face an onslaught next morning. Not one in 10 bothered to replenish his unit's ammunition. Polk withdrew his division a full three miles. Bragg spent the night in Beauregard's tent instead of with his men. No reconnaissance of the enemy was ordered. The Confederates' prize captive, Gen. Prentiss, predicted with a laugh, "It will be very different tomorrow. You'll see. We'll turn the tables on you." Nobody took him seriously, except Nathan Bedford Forrest. He sent out some of his troopers in captured Federal uniforms to scout behind Union lines. From a bluff overlooking the river they saw unit after unit of Buell's army crossing over. Forrest tried to get word to Beauregard but could not find him. When he awoke Hardee to alert him, he was dismissed casually. As dawn broke Federal skirmishers moved forward all along the battle line, followed at a distance by the bulk of Buell's and Grant's armies. There was no firm plan of attack, but soon they found themselves crashing into an enemy unit close to their front line, which, overwhelmed and not expecting an onslaught, fell back firing as they went. Renewed firing elsewhere on the battlefield

A dense wood in the center of the battlelines gave Union soldiers a strong defensive position from which they drove back repeated Confederate charges with such stinging fire that it became known as the Hornet's Nest.

awoke the Confederates, who were still exhausted, hungry, and not expecting to have to fight again. They stumbled out of sleep and hurriedly tried to round up ammunition. Grant was moving 45,000 troops on to the field, half of them fresh. Beauregard could assemble only 20,000 capable of fighting, and they were weary and battered. Grant's men easily retook most of the ground lost the previous day. However, at Shiloh Church, where Beauregard had established his headquarters, they met heavy resistance, the Confederates smashing heavily and desperately against the Federal front. Bragg ordered Brig. Gen. Patrick Cleburne to throw what was left of his men against the Federal salient near the main road to Corinth. Though Cleburne protested that his flank would be left unprotected, Bragg persisted. Before it was over, Cleburne's brigade of 2750 men on Sunday morning was reduced to 1700.

The sheer weight of Federal numbers kept crushing and grinding the enemy units. The situation was hopeless everywhere for the Confederates. In early afternoon the Confederate line was still in front of Shiloh Church, but by 3:30 PM there was nothing to do but withdraw. The men fell in sheer exhaustion after marching only a mile or two. By then, however, the Federals were also spent. Grant issued an order recalling them, and they returned to the ruins of their original camps. There was no pursuit. Next morning, April 8, the battered Confederates set out for Corinth along a narrow road of deep, churned mud. Forrest was guarding the rear with 300 cavalrymen. Sherman was out with four brigades and a cavalry unit making certain the Confederates had cleared the area. Forrest chose to strike. His horsemen dashed among Sherman's skirmishers, and Forrest raced toward Sherman and his main force. Later Sherman said, "I am sure that if Forrest had not emptied his pistols as he passed the skirmish line, my career would have ended right there." It was Forrest who came close to ending his life then and there. Leading the charge he did not see that his men had stopped at the leveled Federal rifles and he was galloping forward alone. He plunged into the Federal line before

Above: *Nathan Bedford Forrest, the demon of Confederate cavalry, was the one man Grant truly dreaded.*

Above right: *General Beauregard, who commanded the firing on Fort Sumter, was no match for Grant at Shiloh.*

he realized his plight. He whirled his horse and tried to cut his way out. A Federal soldier jammed his musket into Forrest's side and fired. The heavy ball lifted Forrest in his saddle and lodged against his spine. Despite the wound, he seized a Federal soldier from the ground, plunked him up on the horse's rump as a shield, and galloped away. He was the last man wounded in the Battle of Shiloh.

The dazed Confederates stumbled down the road to Corinth in a ragged column seven miles or more. An agonizing ordeal – wagons loaded with the wounded piled like bags of grain, mud and water belly-deep, drizzling rain that began at nightfall and became a storm of unrelenting violence with sleet and hail. Corinth was turned into a disaster area of at least 5000 wounded, doctors working until they collapsed from exhaustion, the whole a scene of gangrene and amputations, infection, typhoid.

Back on the Shiloh battlefield the scene was also one of horror. For days teams went out to collect the wounded and dig mass graves for the dead. The bodies lay so close together in places that it would have been possible to walk over them for distances without touching the ground. The

weather turned warm again, and the stench of rotting flesh tainted the air. The casualty totals were appalling. With over 100,000 men involved, each side lost about a quarter of the total troops engaged: for the Union 13,047 casualties out of around 62,682 effectives; for the Confederates about 10,700 of 40,335 effectives. After capturing the heart of the North with the victory at Fort Donelson, Grant was held responsible for the bloody loss of so many of his men at Shiloh. His failure to pursue the Confederates immediately and destroy their armies was seen as reprehensible. He offered no excuses. In a letter to Buell about the possibilities of pursuing Beauregard he implied that he felt constrained by a dispatch from Halleck not to advance beyond "some point which we can reach and return in a day." And Lew Wallace surmised that after the battle Grant was "as much under Halleck's order not to do anything as before it."

The experience of Shiloh, with all its horror, dreadful losses and blunders on both sides, had been one of learning for Grant. He had learned that to defeat the enemy in a battle may not necessarily mean real victory for either side. He had also learned that the war would not be ended by a single swift blow or by negotiation. He knew that the end would not come soon, as had generally been assumed when first the war began. A whole society had to be defeated, the pillaging of civilian property was no longer taboo; rebels within Union lines were to be treated without respect for person or the old rules of war. The concept of what today is called Total War evolved from that realization.

Left: *Under a cloud after the horror of Shiloh, Grant impressed the newspaperman Charles Dana as "of simple manner, straightforward, cordial and umpretending," self-possessed and eager to get on with the war.*

Opposite: *Casualties on both sides at Shiloh totaled close to 24,000, with so many bodies strewn on the battlefield that it appeared a veritable harvest of death requiring teams to work for days collecting the wounded and digging mass graves.*

Below: *Never more confident than in the saddle, Grant (on white horse) galloped from point to point within his lines at Shiloh, encouraging his officers and men in the face of a seemingly hopeless situation.*

Grant had thought Corinth should have been taken immediately. Halleck, instead, who arrived at the front April 11, did not commence his advance until April 30 with a grand army of more than 100,000 men, moving with extreme caution at the rate of a mile a day. By the time he reached Corinth on May 30 the Confederate armies had cleared out. Halleck declared the taking of Corinth a great victory. Actually, it was simply abandoned to the Federal army.

Once again Halleck held back any tribute to Grant for a hard-won battle, even going so far as removing him to a meaningless post, second in command of the armies of the West, which meant a subordinate in Halleck's headquarters. George H. Thomas was given his Army of the Tennessee. Grant was more than discouraged. He asked for a leave of 30 days to go to Covington; he wanted to have time away to consider whether to seek a transfer within the army or resign from it altogether. Sherman, hearing that his friend was planning to leave his command, stepped in. He found Grant in a small encampment of four or five tents, clearly an island of exile. Grant was bundling up letters and about to leave, admitting, "I have stood it as long as I can,

and can endure it no longer." Sherman had no intention of letting that happen. He reminded his friend of his own difficult time, of how he had let himself be driven into a deep depression when a newspaper reporter denounced him as crazy, of fighting back, concluding his argument with "you could not be quiet at home for a week when armies were moving." Grant stayed and waited, not complaining.

Three months after Shiloh, on a July 4 celebration in Memphis, Charles A. Dana, a curious newspaperman whom Stanton had brought into the War Department, went downriver to meet Grant. He knew Grant was under a cloud because of Shiloh. He was pleasantly surprised to find him "a man of simple manner, straightforward, cordial and unpretending," self-possessed and eager to make war. Stanton and Lincoln listened to Dana. In the fall of 1862 Grant was assigned command of the new Federal Department of the Tennessee. Meantime Lincoln decided he wanted Halleck in Washington as general-in-chief, an administrative job that would keep him far from the battlefield. Grant was freed to look down the Mississippi toward Vicksburg and the campaign that could win the war in the West.

The Vicksburg Campaign

Lincoln regarded the opening of the Mississippi as the first and most important of all the Federal military operations. An initial step had been to send Adm. David Glasgow Farragut from Hampton Roads at the beginning of 1862 to take command of the squadron blockading the Gulf Coast. Late in March David Porter, with a force of 20 schooners, joined Farragut and by April 25 the Confederacy had lost its greatest city, New Orleans, with scarcely a real battle. Superior northern engineering and well-mobilized resources made the Union naval forces irresistible. Northern elation over this triumph gave rise to clamor for a victorious advance up the Mississippi. Farragut was ordered to push upstream, and with the aid of Porter's mortar boats got as far as Baton Rouge. But a formidable barrier – Vicksburg – blocked further progress and they had to return to New Orleans. It fell to Grant to find a way to force the evacuation of this heavily fortified Confederate stronghold.

Vicksburg, the Queen of the Mississippi, stood on a high bluff overlooking the river, its batteries ready to dispute the passage of any Union ship. Even today the position looks formidable, but during the Civil War the river followed an entirely different channel. Right at the city it made a great hairpin bend directly under the menacing guns of the defenders. It is extremely difficult for an army to approach it from the north. The line of hills, of which Vicksburg forms a

In early 1863 Admiral David Glasgow Farragut sailed his squadron from Hampton Roads to capture New Orleans, opening the mouth of the Mississippi to Federal gunboats.

part, turns abruptly to the northeast following the Yazoo River. Between these hills and the Mississippi is a vast bottom land known as the Yazoo delta stretching northward for 175 miles. It is 60 miles wide in places and covers an area of several thousand square miles. Most of this land is very soft and very low. If it were not for the levees along the Mississippi it would be under water a great part of the year. Crisscrossed with small streams, large bayous, and rivers, it presented an almost impassable obstacle to a large army with heavy guns and wagons.

On the other side of the Mississippi opposite Vicksburg the bottom land, though not as wide as the Yazoo delta, extends both north and south of the city. The problem confronting an army trying to capture Vicksburg was to reach the high ground east of the Yazoo River or south of the city and assault Vicksburg from the rear. Either solution presented immense difficulties. The first involved crossing the Yazoo delta. The alternative meant finding a way through the bottom land on the opposite bank, then crossing the river to the eastern shore. Supply would be difficult in either case, perhaps impossible by the second method because the supply ships would have to run down past the Vicksburg batteries to reach the troops operating below the city.

Yet if the North was to split the Confederacy into two parts and cut off railroad lines bringing vital supplies from the West to the army in the East, Vicksburg had somehow to be taken. Once Vicksburg was captured the only other important Confederate stronghold guarding the passage on the river, Port Hudson to the south, could be easily taken and the whole river secured. The Confederacy would have no dependable link between its western part – Texas, Arkansas and trans-Mississippi Louisiana – and the remainder.

As Grant turned his full attention to his greatest challenge some strange and disquieting events were occurring in Washington. In September John A. McClernand, the ambitious Illinois politician who had wangled a commission and fought under Grant at Donelson and Shiloh, went to see Lincoln, himself once an ambitious Illinois politician. He proposed recruiting his own forces and personally leading that army in a crushing blow on Vicksburg. Somehow he obtained authorization to proceed to Illinois, Indiana and Iowa and recruit troops and "when a sufficient force, not required by the operations of Gen. Grant's command, shall be raised, an expedition may be organized under Gen. McClernand's command against Vicksburg." Not only was Grant not told of this transaction, neither was Halleck. The news, however, did leak out and reached Grant. He telegraphed Halleck, who, indignant at the mishandling of the whole affair, wired back: "You have command of all troops sent to your dept. and have permission to fight the enemy where you please."

Grant had planned for a single overland thrust on Jackson and Vicksburg. Possibly to thwart McClernand, he decided now on a two-pronged attack, his own overland drive and an amphibious effort by Sherman. Their movements were to be carried out as surreptitiously as possible. However, Confederate intelligence – superior to that of the Union throughout the war – as well as Richmond and Vicksburg

were getting worried about the impending threat. Lt. Gen. John C. Pemberton, who had been put in command at Vicksburg in October, at best a nervous man unsure of himself, began sending desperate pleas for reinforcements. Jefferson Davis, for whom Mississippi was an adopted state and who had a home in Vicksburg, set out by rail at once to inspect the city's defenses. With him was Gen. Joseph E. Johnston, in command of all Confederate forces in the large area between the Appalachians and the Mississippi. Both West Point graduates and each of proven capability in his own way, Davis and Johnston were incompatible to the point of personal enmity. Johnston had accepted the command reluctantly and protested he could not control the extensive area with the numbers of troops Davis grudgingly made available to him. Furthermore, Johnston had a different approach from Pemberton's about how best to defend the city. Pemberton preferred to fight from fixed positions, strongly fortified; Johnston favored movement and mobility that might keep the enemy off balance. Their difference, combined with Davis's attitude toward Johnston, was to affect the fate of Vicksburg.

Resolved to get his troops started whatever McClernand might be doing, Grant worked out his strategy with Sherman, who had all along advocated an expedition down the Mississippi. The Mississippi squadron commander, Adm. David Dixon Porter, delighted at the prospect of sharing in the expedition, assembled a flotilla at the mouth of the Yazoo River north of Vicksburg for the purpose of destroying Confederate batteries and mines and setting up landing areas for Sherman's troops. But the Confederates had gotten ahead of him. Some innovative officer named Beverly Kennon had been experimenting with an electrically activated torpedo, or mine, and had come to Vicksburg in the

David Porter's mortar boats enabled Union naval forces to push upstream from New Orleans as far as Baton Rouge, but checked there because of the Confederate stronghold at Vicksburg. They were later to have a critical role in freeing access to the heavily fortified city.

fall of 1862 to guide in anchoring the device strategically in the channel of the Yazoo. When in December the Federal squadron of five vessels steamed up the Yazoo, the ironclad *Cairo*, one of its proudest, struck the device and within 12 minutes was at the bottom of the river (the first recorded incident in naval annals in which a warship had been sunk on contact with a mine).

On the day of this disaster Sherman, with two additional forces McClernand had sent ahead to Memphis, was moving south on the river to a point where the Yazoo River enters the Mississippi at Chickasaw Bluffs. Meanwhile, Grant moved his forces overland, first to the garrison and supply depot at Holly Springs and then south to Oxford. On December 10, while at Oxford, 3500 gray-clad horsemen led by Mississippian Earl Van Dorn, head of Pemberton's cavalry, swept into Holly Springs with the spine-tingling Rebel yell first heard at Manassas. Most of the garrison was captured before having time to fall in line, then the raiders put the torch to ammunition dumps, provision depots, trains and storage sheds, sending up in smoke some $1,500,000 worth of supplies essential to Grant's continuance of his campaign.

There was more bad news to come. Nathan Bedford Forrest, the demon of Confederate cavalry, raided Union communication lines in western Tennessee. Forrest was the one man Grant sincerely dreaded because he was amenable to no known rules of procedure, a law to himself for all military acts, constantly showing up at all times and places with the unexpected. He led his 2500 peerless horsemen across lower Tennessee, routed opposing Federal troops near Lexington, struck railroad lines between Jackson, Tennessee, and Columbus, Kentucky, burning bridges, trestles, depots, tearing up 60 miles of track and tearing down all telegraph wires on the route. Together with Van Dorn's raid at Holly Springs he stopped Grant's advance toward Vicksburg. Because of the cutting of communications, Grant was unable to get word of this disaster to Sherman, who continued his downriver drive, confident that when he reached Vicksburg Grant would have taken care of Pemberton and would be waiting with his army for the final, critical assault.

Grant had no choice but to pull back to Grand Junction. He was in enemy territory, the Mississippians gloating at his plight, his supplies destroyed. He found a solution exceeding his expectations. He sent out guarded wagons by the scores for 25 miles on both sides of the road to scour the country for food and flour. Mills were erected, grain ground, stock driven in and slaughtered. When asked by the inhabi-

Below: *Map showing Union and Confederate positions in final siege of Vicksburg, and the topographical difficulties encountered.*

Right: *Confederate General Joseph E. Johnston was held back by the enmity of Jefferson Davis from action that might have saved Vicksburg.*

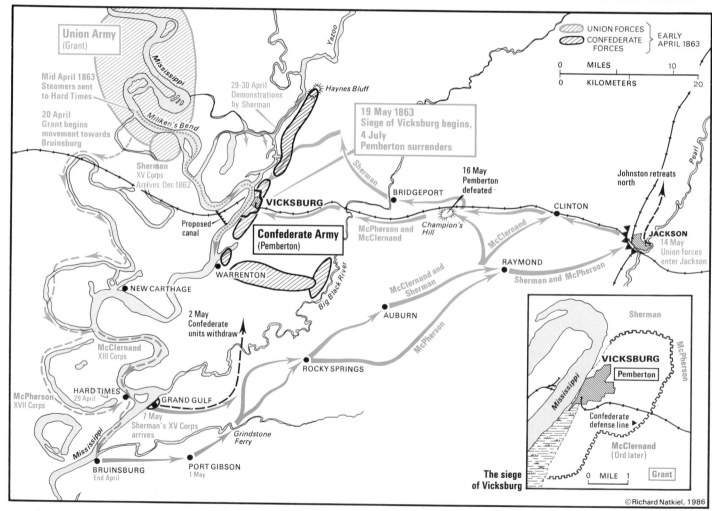

Left: *Lincoln's Emancipation Proclamation of January 1, 1863, was the most important document in the history of freedom in America since the Declaration of Independence, and established unequivocably his presidential and personal authority.*

Inset below: *In a vist to a Union camp, Lincoln was accompanied by Allan Pinkerton (to his left), a private detective who helped set up a Secret Service branch for the U.S. Army, and by Major General John McClernand, a vainglorious Illinois politician who clashed with Grant's authority at Vicksburg.*

tants what they themselves should live on, he advised them to move farther south. He would not allow his army to starve so long as there was anything within reach to feed them. To his amazement quantities of supplies were so abundant within this narrow zone alone that he found he could sustain his force for two months. It was an important lesson he was to remember later in the campaign.

Withdrawing to Memphis he tried unsuccessfully to get word to Sherman. Forrest's raiders had also torn down wire communications to the rear. Unknown to Grant, the Confederates had at their disposal a private telegraph wire

along the west bank of the river north of Vicksburg linked to a post at Lake Providence 42 miles north of Vicksburg. From there the Federal gunboats and transports were spotted, and word quickly passed on in time for the Confederates to muster reinforcements and prepare for Sherman when he landed his men on the south bank of the Yazoo northwest of Chickasaw Bluffs. Once Sherman had led his divisions through the boggy stretch of swamps and bayous to a position of assault, Confederate cannon were ready for him. Though the attack was fierce, it was easily repulsed with severe Union losses, their casualties totaling 1776; those of

A raid by Earl Van Dorn and his Confederate cavalry wiped out Grant's base at Holly Springs, Miss., cutting him off from communications and leaving him in enemy territory to feed his men by living off the land.

the Confederates were only 187. After planning an attack farther upstream at Haines Bluff the next morning, Sherman was driven by heavy fog and rain to fall back to Milliken's Bend on the Mississippi.

It was at this point that McClernand turned up and in a towering rage showed Sherman his orders from the President placing him in command of his self-styled "Army of the Mississippi." Kowtowing to McClernand was a bitter pill for Sherman to swallow, but in view of his rank, which was junior to McClernand's, he moved as agreeably as he could to the role of corps commander. Seeing that McClernand had no real plan to offer, he suggested moving 20 miles up the Arkansas River to Fort Hindman, better known as the Post of Arkansas, held by some 5000 Confederates under Brig. Gen. Thomas S. Churchill. McClernand grabbed at the idea, thinking this would establish his authority as *de facto* head of the Army of the Mississippi. Adm. Porter thoroughly disliked McClernand, and it took much persuasion on Sherman's part to get his cooperation in assigning the necessary gunboats to McClernand. This time Sherman did his own re-

connoitering and made sure of his ground and the exact situation at the fort.

By the morning of January 11, 1863, the gunboats were bombarding from the river and Sherman's corps advancing under heavy fire. But the combined effort, the gunboats supplemented by the attacking troops, worked. A large white flag went up on the ramparts. In casualties it was a mixed victory. The Federal attacking force suffered a total of 1063 (140 killed and 923 wounded); the Confederates, on the other hand, had only 109 men hit, but 4791 were taken captive. Though it had in fact been Sherman's and Porter's operation, McClernand, at a safe haven on a gunboat, was jubilant, shouting "Glorious! Glorious! My star is ever in the ascendant." Straightaway he wrote Grant proposing that he penetrate deeper into Arkansas.

Grant was furious. This was a deviation from the prime objective – the capture of Vicksburg. Furthermore, with communications now restored, he learned from the indignant Sherman and Porter what had really taken place. In the interim he had received from Halleck what he wanted, a wire authorizing him "to relieve Gen. McClernand from command of the expedition against Vicksburg, giving it to the next in rank or taking it yourself." Grant ordered McClernand to Milliken's Bend, where he met him and made clear that he was in command. McClernand complained to Lincoln with wild accusations and vituperation, but Lincoln, already advised by Halleck of the situation, judiciously advised him to confine his attention to the common goal of Union harmony and victory.

Now at last there was clearly a single general whose control extended over both banks of the river, including a piece of Arkansas and Louisiana, and who had the unqualified support of Lincoln and Halleck, the approval of Porter, the undivided loyalty of Sherman. At the end of January 1863 the real work of the campaign of Vicksburg could begin.

Another event of that first month of 1863 was to have a profound impact on Grant's campaign for Vicksburg and on the outcome of the war. It was Lincoln's Emancipation Proclamation of January 1, 1863. To a North still politically at odds on the question of slavery, it established the fact that Lincoln was in charge of the running of the war and all that involved – military, economic, moral. He had established his presidential and personal authority.

Since Grant's first attempt to capture Vicksburg by a combined land and water action had failed, he had to devise other ways of crossing the Yazoo delta or bypassing the city. Conditions that winter and spring of 1863 made any plan dubious. In such low, swampy country, with winter rains and chilly weather, finding any dry land was next to impossible, and the wetness pervading everything – clothing, tents, bedding – was conducive to outbreaks of malaria and smallpox among the troops. Nevertheless, he was resolved that to suspend activities and simply winter over idly would only invite delays and complications.

A number of plans would be made and attempted in those months of the spring of 1863, and not all would have even a degree of success. The first of these efforts – digging a canal across the narrow neck of land opposite the city – was undertaken primarily because Lincoln, who had once made a trip down-river on a flatboat, was set on the idea that the short neck of land where the river looped up to Vicksburg then curved back to within five miles of itself could be breached. Grant had no genuine expectations of such a venture, but it was a way to keep his men busy. Much of the digging was done by hand, though dredges were also used. Eventually Confederate artillery across the river was trained on two dredge barges. By then it was evident that in any case the canal was not deep enough to achieve its purpose of providing a new channel of the river, and the work was stopped.

Another canal project, known as the Lake Providence Route, was strictly one of construction, cutting a canal from the Mississippi into Lake Providence on its west side, then finding passages through bayous and rivers for 200 miles south to Red River, a lengthy detour to Vicksburg. It was abandoned when it proved impossible to cut through the stumps of trees under water and dense overhanging branches. The intention of these plans was to open a channel for the fleet to pass below the city without having to run beneath the storming of the batteries atop its strong fortifications.

Two efforts to cross the delta – the Yazoo Pass Route and the Steele's Bayou Route – held more promise. A levee was cut at Yazoo Pass some 300 miles upstream and transports sent toward the upper reaches of the Yazoo River, a long and winding stretch. The gunboats and ironclads made it as far as Fort Pemberton, whose commander was Brig. Gen. Lloyd Tilghman, who had fired at Federal gunboats at Fort Henry. He had a second chance now, though the fort was not heavily equipped with guns. But it was nature, not his insufficiency of guns, that spared him a second surrender. The country around the fort was under water so that the troops could not march on land, and the channel so narrow the boats could not maneuver, and there was nothing for them to do but turn back.

An attempt to reach the upper Yazoo by way of Steele's Bayou Route combined naval forces under the command of

Adm. Porter himself and Gen. Sherman following on land with parts of his corps. To make even four miles a day Porter had to knock down trees, pull up roots, tear his way through bridges with his ironclads. His flagship had barely been freed from a bed of willows when the Confederates closed in and began felling trees in the rear of the ships so that they could not turn around. Sharpshooters lined the bank to shoot anyone who showed himself on deck. Porter managed to get a call for help to Sherman, who paddled a canoe through swampland to round up extra forces for the rescue. They arrived just in time to save Porter and his fleet from capture by the Confederates. It took four more days to disentangle the fleet and get the ships backed out to a place wide enough to turn around.

By April it was obvious to Grant that none of these operations would get him to Vicksburg, and he proceeded to stake everything on a final hazardous plan of campaign. He would march down the west bank of the Mississippi, cross the river below Vicksburg, and there, with only supplies that could be taken with the troops, abandon his line of communications and thus all hope of resupply in case of defeat. Adm. Porter enthusiastically agreed to do his part, which was to get his fleet somehow past the batteries of Vicksburg to a point safely below the city where he could assist Grant's army across the river to the Vicksburg side.

Sherman was temporarily left near Vicksburg to demon-

Grant's headquarters on the Mississippi above Vicksburg, where one of his plans for crossing the river failed when high waters broke the levees, drowned out the camps, and flooded the country.

IMPORTANT FROM AMERICA!!
Awful Slaughter at Vicksburg,
And Elsewhere,
The Bloody Conflict between the North & South
CONTINUED!

We regret to say that this unnatural war seems still to rush upon the unhappy Yanky with fearful impetuosity, so as to stun the entire population and saturate the States of America with blood, by sacrificing the lives of hundreds of thousands of honest men, at the whim or caprice of a few noxious individuals. Federal accounts state that the siege still continues, —and, that the incredible number of 3,600 bombs were thrown into the city of Vicksburg in an hour! The streets are ploughed up with shot and shell, and that the inhabitants dwell in caves which they have excavated in the sides of the Bluff!

In the force under Banks and Sheridan there was a battalion of Negroes, who are said to have fought well. They suffered terribly, for out of a regiment of 900, 600 were killed or wounded in an hour!

The Prize Court at Key West has laid down the law of confiscation so as to insure the condemnation of every British Ship a Federal vessel may seize,—'Any vessel bound to Nassau, with the intention of sailing from thence to a blockaded port, is liable to condemnation." As the prize court constitutes inself sole judge of the intention, and as Matamoras has been, de facto blockaded, all British vessels bound for that port will, of course, be at once condemned. The Key west correspondent of the New-York Herald has good reason to say that "nowhere else is prise law rigidly enforced, vessels being condemned at the rate of two each week."

Although 49,688 emigrants had arrived in New York from Ireland since the first of January, 1863, and though the negroes are said to be the "best hope of restoring the Union," the enrollment is being enforced.

Queenstown, Saturday.—The following is the latest "correspondence" from Vicksburg. One regiment only, the 22nd Iowa Volunteers, commanded by Colonel William M. Stone, by almost superhuman efforts, and after immense loss, planted its colours on the rebal rampart. There it remained all day long, the colonel hourly demanding aid, until at nightfall, after having been exposed all day to a destructive fire, the lieutenant-colonel and 15 men only remained and they were taken in great triumph to Vicksburg. Every man who entered the fort in the morning was killd or wounded except these sixteen. Colonel Stone was struck in the arm whilst on the bastion, loudly calling for reinforcements. It was a stupid blunder, or worse, to storm the works at all. It needs not a military eye to discover that it is impossible to lead men over an abrupt embankment twenty feet high, with ditchos from ten to twelve feet deep. It was doubtless, necessary that the experiment should be tried. It has proven a costly one. Twenty-five hundred killed and wounded is a fearful loss.

The northerns are evidently constructing a new line of works between the outer line opposed to us and the city. While the charge was being made on the 22nd some of our sharpshooters, posted in the trees overlooking the fortifications, could plainly see contrabands and white men digging for dear life.

OUR LOSSES.

I regret to learn that Colonel Abbet, of the 30th Iowa, was killed on the 22nd instant. He was a brave officer, and his loss is universally regretted. In the battle of Champion's Hill, on the 16th, instant, the tenth Iowa lost, killed, wounded, and missing, one hundred and sixty-one men. Among the killed were three commissioned officers and 7 wounded. In the recent charge on the fortifications the twenty-second Iowa, lost two hundred and fifty men ; General Stevenson's Brigade, two hundred and sixty ; General Ransom's Brigade, three hundred and fifty-eight. General Carr's division, five hundred ; General Blair's division, five hundred and fifty ; Gereyal Steele's division, heavily, estimated six hundred ; General Osterhaus' division two hundred, estimated ; and General Smith's three hundred and fifty, estimated. This is rather under than over the estimate.

CANNONADING.

To-day there has been vigorous cannonading at intervals from batteries on the right and left of the railroad. A misdirected shot fell in our own ranks killing three soldiers of the thirty-second Ohio, and seriously wounding as many more.

Over one hundred women and children have been killed by our bombardment.

New-York, June 14—General Banks flicially reports that the conduct of the Negro troops has been most praiseworthy, and there is no longer any doubt that the Government will find in the Negroes effective supporters.

General Banks' loss from the 28rd to the 30th, ult., was 1,000 men, including many of his ablest officers.

General Sherman has died of his wounds.

General Neal Dow is also dangerously wounded.

ANOTHER BATTLE.

Three brigades of Federal Cavalry, and 2,000 Infantry crossed the Rappahannock on Tuesday at Beverley Ford, and had a severe engagement with General Stuart's cavalry, lasting all day, when the Confederates received heavy infantry reinforcements, and the Federals recrossed the river bringing away their dead and wounded. Sharp firing was kept up from the confederate rifle pits during the crossing, and 40 of the Federals were killed or weunded. A portion of Federal land and naval farces at Yorktown, made an incursion into King William Country. Virginia, via the Mattapony River. On the 4th inst. a Foundry at Ayltes, with all its machinery, several mills, and large quantities of grain, were destroyed, and many horses, mules, and cattle were captured. The expedition returned to Yorktown the following day.

The agricultural resources of the Yazoo country are described as being most abundant

John F. Nugent and Co., Steam-Machine Printers, 35, New-Row West, Dublin. N.B.—No connection with any other person of the name.

strate against the city when the time came and confuse the Confederates about Grant's intentions. To confuse the Confederate forces further Col. Benjamin H. Grierson was to head a raid with his large force of cavalry through Mississippi into Louisiana, joining Union forces there. He carried out the assignment magnificently, spreading alarm and excitement everywhere, and diverting attention away from Grant's operation.

On the night of April 16 Adm. Porter carried out the first stage of the plan in an event made memorable by a famous Currier & Ives print. He had made his preparations with great care, piling the sides of transports with cotton, hay, and grain, and strengthening the ironclads with logs. Under the spectacular two-and-a-half hour bombardment from the heights of Vicksburg, amid fiery flares from huge barrels of tar set ablaze to light the scene for the defenders of Vicksburg, he drifted his ships down with the current to a point safely below the city to await Grant's army. On April 30, at a crossing point nine miles south of Grand Gulf, the Union forces, 31,000 strong, started across the Mississippi. They were unopposed.

The following day Union forces easily and decisively defeated resistance at Port Gibson, which was inadequate to the threat. Pemberton had been badly thrown off by Grierson's raid and the damage it caused. He hesitated to

Left: *Sentiment in Britain and Ireland was in general more favorable to the South than to the North. A Dublin newspaper report at time of Vicksburg noting the thousands of Irish immigrants enlisted to fight in the "awful slaughter."*

Top: *Rear Admiral David Dixon Porter, highly skilled commander of the Union Mississippi Squadron, provided invaluable assistance in the Vicksburg campaign.*

Right: *Union forces tried for months to cut a canal across a narrow neck of land opposite Vicksburg to open passage for Federal gunboats, but spring flooding and Confederate artillery from across the river forced the project to be discontinued.*

A levee at Vicksburg thronged with Mississippi steamboats, the major source of supplies up and down the river and vital to both North and South. Once the river was reopened to shipping from Minnesota to the Gulf of Mexico, the West was essentially lost to the Confederacy.

weaken the garrison at Port Hudson, just above Baton Rouge, in part because Jefferson Davis had repeatedly stressed its importance. Appeals to Johnston for reinforcements were unavailing. Besides, it was already rapidly becoming too late for the Confederates to have saved Vicksburg if ever they really could have done so in view of Grant's superior forces, resources available, and adroit pertinacity.

Grant was not, however, to have his prize with a single smashing blow. It would take two more months of maneuvering his troops back and forth, at times abandoning even his own supply lines and lines of communication as he moved closer, ever closer to Vicksburg.

By May 3 the Confederates had evacuated Grand Gulf after the Union army crossed the river at Hard Times Landing on the west bank of Bruinsberg and their victory at Port Gibson. Moving up to the rear of Vicksburg from the southwest, Grant placed his vast army within a pincers formed by Pemberton in Vicksburg and Johnston, now in control of Jackson, Mississippi, east of the city. His object was to cut the Vicksburg-Jackson railroad. Sherman's troops were ordered to Jackson, which was taken on May 14. Meantime, though Pemberton put up a vigorous defense at Champion's Hill, an assault by the forces of McClernand and James B. McPherson won the day. From there, under Grant's watchful eye, the Confederates were driven back across the Big Black River.

It was in the midst of these decisive operations that a staff officer rode up and handed Grant instructions that had been sent May 11 from Halleck. They ordered him to return to Grand Gulf and cooperate from there with Gen. Nathaniel P. Banks, who had come up from his command post at New Orleans for the siege of Confederate-held Port Hudson, then combine their forces for the final attack on Vicksburg. At that moment Grant heard great cheering to the right of his line and saw one of his brigade commanders in his shirt sleeves leading a charge upon the enemy. He quickly mounted his horse and rode in the direction of the charge, leaving the messenger who had brought the dispatch un-

answered. It was a deliberate act of that insubordination for which Halleck had once severely reproached him. But now he was confident both in himself and in Halleck's trust that the course he had taken was right. Throughout these critical days, as the long drawn-out siege neared its climax, Grant is described by one observer as standing cool and calculating with a cigar in his mouth, issuing orders for assaults in the midst of the most heated fighting over bloody ground. Even when nothing seemed to be going well, he acted as though that was to be expected, and went on sending fresh troops in to buck things up.

From the last weeks of May on through June, assault after assault failed to break the Vicksburg defenses. Pemberton, a trained engineer, had erected earthworks difficult to pierce. One assault resulted in relieving Grant of at least one aggravation he had had to contend with, Gen. McClernand. Because of McClernand's rank, political backing, and undeniable willingness to fight, Grant had felt compelled to make use of him and his corps. In an assault on May 22 he caused Grant to believe he might be making a breakthrough, and appealed to him to have Sherman's and McPherson's men take up a second attack. Though doubtful, Grant felt he could not afford to ignore the request in case his subordinate's claims of his near-success might just happen to be correct. On Grant's orders Sherman sent out a brigade spearheaded by the 11th Missouri at one point, and McPherson launched an assault at another. The Missourians were mowed down by the score, and McPherson's assault got nowhere. By nightfall McClernand pulled his troops back. When, shortly thereafter, Grant directed him to send some troops to watch the crossings of the Big Black River, he swore at the officer delivering the order and denounced Grant in the strongest language, refusing to be dictated to by General Grant. A couple of weeks later he wrote an order of congratulations to his corps, slighting the efforts of the other corps, and saw that his headquarters leaked it to the newspapers. This violated a standing War Department regulation requiring that such papers be submitted to army headquarters before publication. The order was really intended, of course, to impress McClernand's constituency in Illinois.

For Grant it was the last straw. He promptly relieved McClernand of his command. No one was sorry to see him go, including his own corps. When Lincoln received McClernand's protest against his dismissal, he shrugged it off with the comment that should future events prove him right, he would thereby be exonerated, one way for an experienced Illinois politician to relegate another to oblivion. By then Lincoln was betting the future of his presidency and of the country on another man from Illinois – Ulysses S. Grant.

As the month of June dragged on, Grant's men continuously built and rebuilt trenches around Vicksburg, his line extending 15 miles. And the Confederates as continuously reinforced their earthwork fortifications. Frequently the

two sides were so close they exchanged talk and games when they were not trying to kill each other. It was a true instance of brother fighting brother, for there were men on both sides from Missouri, a state divided in its loyalties, here facing one another across only a few yards as foes.

Conditions in Vicksburg by this time were wretched beyond human endurance. No one could get in or out of the beleaguered city, and neither could food. Many holed up in caves dug into the hills. The standard diet was mule meat, dried peas, and even fried rat. Ammunition was low. Yet day after day the guns fired on.

All along Grant had resorted to his engineers to formulate plans of attack to be carried out as circumstances warranted. One of the engineering projects had put the men to work digging tunnels and mining them. On June 25 a mine blew off the top of a hill, creating a crater into which an assaulting column could charge (a technique used later on

Left: *The high bluff on which Vicksburg was situated made an approach impossible from the river. Grant finally resolved the dilemma by crossing south of the city, moving up to its rear and holding it siege by cutting all escape and supply routes by land in and out.*

Left: *Admiral Porter's fleet running the blockade of the Mississippi at Vicksburg the night of April 16, 1863, amid concentrated fire from atop the bluff and blazing floats of combustible materials set loose in the channel through which the ships passed.*

a grander scale at Petersburg). Behind a parapet previously constructed, the Confederates fought back so fiercely that their attackers had to be recalled. Time after time mines were exploded, and each time the attacking Union soldiers were repulsed.

Grant set the date of July 6 for the final onslaught, a date he never had to keep. Pemberton could not expect deliverance from Johnston, who was tied up on the Big Black River hoping vainly to distract the Army of the Tennessee. The consensus of his generals when he asked if their men could stand a battle and long hard march was in the negative. At 10:30 AM on July 3 he sent two horsemen under a flag of truce to the Union lines. One of them was Gen. John Bowen, an old friend of Grant's in St. Louis, sent in the hope that their personal relationship would induce Grant to grant an armistice and agree to a commission to work out a formula for surrender. Grant did not see him. As at Fort Donelson his terms were simple and unequivocal – total surrender of the city and garrison. At 3 PM Pemberton rode out with Bowen and a staff officer to see what he could do. The two generals, who had served together in the Mexican War, walked away to a stunted oak tree, and sat down face to face. With his characteristic quiet firmness and in a few simple, direct words, Grant made it clear that he had nothing more to say than what he had said in his letter. By 10 o'clock that evening the final terms were worked out with his division commanders in the area and sent to Pemberton.

Although the "total surrender" stipulation remained, Grant did ease it slightly by proposing that after the garrison forces gave up their arms, they would be released on parole, meaning they must not engage in further action in

Above: *On July 3, 1863, Grant received a message from Confederate General Pemberton requesting a formula for surrender of Vicksburg.*

Below: *Lieutenant General John C. Pemberton was a Northerner who joined the Confederate army and was chosen by Jefferson Davis to defend Vicksburg.*

the war. In addition, they would be allowed to keep their side arms and swords, as well as their mounts. Though later criticized by some in the North for granting paroles, Grant and his fellow officers saw that transporting some 30,000 prisoners up the Mississippi would tie up Porter's fleet indefinitely, as well as incur the burden of taking care of that many prisoners. It was not to humiliate brave men that Grant had come to Vicksburg – it was to remove the main block on the Mississippi River. The inevitable fall of Port Hudson five days later opened the river completely to Union shipping all the way to New Orleans.

On the morning of July 4, 1863, white flags waved over the now silent Confederate Vicksburg fortifications, and over the city's courthouse the Confederate flag was lowered and the Stars and Stripes raised in its place. From that day to July 4, 1945, after the Allied victory in Europe made the nation truly united, Vicksburg never again officially celebrated Independence Day.

On that morning, also, in far-off Pennsylvania, Robert E. Lee began his return from the ravaged fields of Gettysburg after three unforgettable days of battle. Gettysburg marked the first critically decisive defeat for the South and its beloved general. Vicksburg marked the first truly decisive victory for the North and the general who until then had known more reviling than respect. That day it was not the Philadelphia patrician George Gordon Meade, victor at Gettysburg, who was hailed as hero across the North. It was the small-town tanner's son and failed farmer, Ulysses S. Grant.

Throughout the month of June 1863 Union divisions encircled Vicksburg in a line extending 15 miles, continuously reinforcing their earthwork fortifications, and building and rebuilding trenches in preparation for a final onslaught they never had to carry out. Surrender came first.

The Chattanooga Campaign

Grant spent the next two months in Vicksburg with Julia and their four children in a house high on the bluff. He had wanted to move his men quickly through southern Mississippi into Alabama and take Mobile, but Washington had another priority. Lincoln was eager to hold Chattanooga, the last vital city of the Confederacy, in the southeastern corner of Tennessee near the borders of Alabama and Georgia on the banks of the Tennessee River. A small town of 3500 people, it was an important strategic location, intersecting railroad lines and sources of supply for the Confederate armies.

What was happening those two months in and around Chattanooga was not in the least pleasant for Gen. William S. Rosecrans and his Federal Army of the Cumberland. Since the first of the year he was more or less stalled in central Tennessee with Confederate Gen. Braxton Bragg's army no more than 30 miles away. His object was to keep Bragg sufficiently tied up to prevent his joining Pemberton in Vicksburg. Now the time had come to move.

The approaches to Chattanooga were difficult. West of the city mountainous terrain defended the Tennessee Val-

ley on both sides. North and south of it was a range of mountains with Lookout Mountain, 2000 feet above sea level and 30 miles long, in the middle, then, east of it, Missionary Ridge and Pigeon Hill, which could be crossed only through narrow passes. Finally, in August, Rosecrans managed, by getting his army below the city, to come up from the south with the object of entrapping the Confederates so that they would have to fight their way out, starve, or surrender. Instead, Bragg evacuated the city before Rosecrans could get there, creating the illusion of fleeing in disarray. What he was really doing was reshuffling his four divisions, supplemented by reinforcements that arrived from Gen. Johnston's army and a corps of 12,000 under Lt. Gen. James Longstreet, one of Lee's top generals.

Interpreting Bragg's "flight" as retreat, Rosecrans pursued him with three corps in a right, center, left formation under three generals, among them George H. Thomas and Thomas L. Crittenden. At daybreak September 19 the Confederates opened their attack on Chickamauga Creek about 12 miles below Chattanooga. To the Union forces the battlefield, its front line stretching some six miles through dense-

Ulysses S. Grant and his wife, the former Julia Dent, with their four children: Frederick (in cadet's uniform) and Nellie standing, Ulysses Jr. ("Buck") seated, and Jesse, the youngest, in foreground with croquet mallet.

ly wooded territory, was ever after remembered as a place of unimaginable bloody horror. Chickamauga, in Cherokee, means "river of death." For the men of both sides who fought there that day it was that, and more. Though it was a victory for the Confederates, their casualties were nearly a third of their original army, the Union losses about the same.

Of the generals in command, the performance of neither was distinguished. Bragg's reputation was not enhanced, Rosecrans's was wrecked. But of those leading a division under Rosecrans one did make a name. After withdrawing to Chattanooga, Rosecrans sent a messenger to George H. Thomas, who was still fighting on, ordering him to leave the field with his men. "It will ruin the army if we withdraw now," was Thomas's reply. In reporting back to Rosecrans the messenger said of Thomas that he was "standing like a rock." For the rest of his life, for all time, Thomas would be known as the "Rock of Chickamauga."

In the second week of October, still in Vicksburg, Grant received a mysterious communication from Halleck to go to Cairo, Illinois, and from there report by telegraph to Washington. At Cairo he learned he was to go to Louisville at once to meet with an officer in the War Department who was bringing him orders. That "officer" was Secretary of War Edwin Stanton. This was their first meeting. The orders were that Grant was to be head of a new military division of the Mississippi, combining the Armies of the Tennessee, the Cumberland, and Ohio. In the case of the Army of the Cumberland, Grant was given two sets of orders to choose from, one leaving Rosecrans in command, the other George H. Thomas. It was Thomas whom Halleck had named to re-

Top: *Union Lieutenant Van Pelt defends his battery in combat at Chickamauga, September 1863.*

Above: *Confederate General Braxton Bragg was victorious at Chickamauga but lost Chattanooga – and his command.*

Overleaf: *Chattanooga, a small town on the banks of the Tennessee River, was an important strategic location, intersecting railroad lines and sources of supply for the Confederacy. Lincoln was bent on wresting control of it from the South's hold.*

B-7043

about the job and has left us a detailed description: He wrote swiftly, never pondering a word or phrase, seldom making a correction. When he finished a page he pushed it off the table on to the floor and went on to the next. Once he finished, he simply picked up all the pages, sorted them like an automatic filing clerk, ready for distribution to the individuals who were to carry out the orders they contained.

One of these orders summoned William Tecumseh Sherman to bring his Army of the Tennessee east from Corinth. Gen. Joseph Hooker – "Fighting Joe," whose star had waned since Lee's magnificent victory over the Army of the Potomac at Chancellorsville in May 1863 – was brought west from the Rappahannock in Virginia. With a fresh supply of several thousand men, he was told to hold his force ready on the north bank of the Tennessee not far from Brown's Ferry, downstream from Chattanooga, where pontoon bridges were to be built to bring supplies across the river. The Civil War was the first in which railroads were used effectively for military purposes, transporting men and supplies with comparative speed long distances. For Grant, with the wide terrain under his command, they were indispensable to success.

Among the officers on Thomas's staff who had presented their reviews the night of Grant's arrival was an engineer, Gen. William F. Smith, whom he had known at West Point. Smith was responsible for bridges and roads, and his review had so impressed Grant that he promptly assigned him the task of "opening up the cracker line" for ammunition, food, and clothing, all in short supply. Nowhere before, or perhaps after, was Grant's organization and marshaling of forces so concentrated or challenging as it was when he stepped into the trap Chattanooga had become. Confederate forces occupied the two prominent mountain ranges and the valley between them. On the right flank, southeast of the city, was Missionary Ridge, rising 200 feet above the plain and heavily defended by Confederate troops at the crest, the middle of the slope, and the foot of the ridge. The scenically impressive rugged slopes of Lookout Mountain rose 1500 feet above the plain on the southwest of the city, a formidable Confederate stronghold affording an all-encompassing view of the river where it makes a U-shaped bend. When Sherman arrived November 15 and surveyed the heavily fortified scene, he said to Grant, "You are besieged," to which there was but one answer, "It is too true."

On high ground in the plain in front of Missionary Ridge on the river side was Orchard Knob, a Confederate outpost line. It was there Grant started his attack on November 23 with Thomas's Army of the Cumberland, who captured it that day. Ordering reinforcements and entrenchments there, Grant made it his command post the next day. While Sherman's forces were crossing a new pontoon bridge across the river to the north to advance toward Missionary Ridge, Hooker with his men from the Army of the Potomac stormed up Lookout Mountain in what was to become known as "The Battle above the Clouds" because the top was enshrouded in heavy fog. The Confederate forces were less numerous than supposed, Hooker's outnumbering them six to one. On November 25, at dawn, the Stars and Stripes were planted at the summit.

The next focus of attack was Missionary Ridge, scheduled for that day. Grant's orders were for Sherman to capture the north end of the Ridge on the right while Hooker kept Bragg from reinforcing his flanks south of Lookout Mountain. But Sherman miscalculated his position, attacked too far north,

Above: *Union General William S. Rosecrans, who forced Bragg back at Stone's River, Tenn., was defeated at Chickamauga.*

Opposite page: *Portrait by W. C. Wyeth of Grant astride a horse and gazing from under the brim of a battered hat.*

place Grant as commander of the Army of the Tennessee in that dark time after Shiloh when Grant had come close to resigning from the army. In addition to that unhappy association, he knew Thomas to be slow to act, methodical, stubborn. But he also considered Rosecrans as less reliable. He chose Thomas.

Learning next day that Rosecrans was about to abandon Chattanooga, Grant began action at once on what was to be the most dramatically spectacular and certainly most splendidly panoramic battle of the war. It started by Thomas's famous reply to Grant's wire to hold Chattanooga at all costs: "We will hold till we starve." Grant joined Thomas at nightfall October 22. The final stage of the journey had been hazardous, for the railroad ended at Bridgeport, Ala., which meant traveling on horseback for several days over a steep, narrow, rocky mountain road often through heavy rain and always and everywhere mud. At one point Grant's horse slipped and threw him, badly bruising his leg. Upon arriving at the small house serving as Thomas's headquarters, he dismissed offers of dry clothes and sat down to hear the reviews of the precarious situation by staff officers. Thereupon he started writing out orders and dispatches covering the whole spectrum of problems and needs. As he worked that evening and into the night, one of his aides, Horace Porter, observed how he went

and was held at bay for more than eight hours by Confederate defenders under the tough Irish division commander Pat Cleburne. Although Hooker responded with alacrity and had his troops at Chattanooga Creek by noon, he found that the Confederates had partially destroyed the bridge over the flooded stream, and was held up for three hours making repairs to get his infantry and artillery across. Thomas's Army of the Cumberland in the center was kept back from action to allow these other operations to go forward as planned – feeling left out of things, resentful of Grant's slights and the way Hooker's Easterners and Sherman's veterans always looked down on them.

From his command post on Orchard Knob Grant had a full view of the entire field, including the crest of Missionary Ridge almost directly in front of him, and of Bragg's headquarters just beyond. By 3 PM, with Sherman stalled and Hooker delayed, he finally gave orders for the Army of the Cumberland to take the rifle pits at the foot of Missionary Ridge and wait there for further instructions. He intended it as a diversionary tactic only, to relieve pressure on Sherman, for his confidence in Thomas's army was limited. Then something happened that was not scheduled. Having taken the rifle pits, the men of the much maligned Army of the Cumberland simply took matters into their own hands. They started up the steep face of the ridge, each battalion with a color-bearer, who would dash ahead of the line. If he fell under the killing fire from above, the flag would be snatched up by the next man, and if he too fell, grabbed again and waved defiantly. When asked by Grant if he had given orders for the men to go forward, Gen. Gordon Granger, one of the heroes of the Chickamauga disaster and in command of the attacking corps, admitted he had not, but added, "When those fellows get started all hell can't stop them." He was right. Crying "Chickamauga! Chickamauga!" they forged on under a hail of musket balls pouring down on them from the top. An hour after the forward surge began, Thomas's men were on the crest of the ridge, the Confederates in headlong flight. Gen. Philip Sheridan's cavalrymen swept up the slope and across the summit of Missionary Ridge, routing what remained of the Confederate defenders and capturing many prisoners. (Within a year Sheridan was to demonstrate far more devastatingly his doggedness for pursuing and ravaging whatever lay in his path.)

Bragg tried in vain to rally his force. Grant did not consider it worth going after his beaten foe. And Bragg was beaten; he was relieved as general of the Army of Tennessee.

Chattanooga was now won, and it was time to tie up loose ends and move on to other fields. Grant sent Sherman's exhausted men on a grueling 85-mile march to bring support and supplies to Ambrose Burnside and his Union Army of the Ohio, whose hold on Knoxville was under threat of an attack. It turned out to be an easier assignment than anticipated. Upon learning of Sherman's approach, Longstreet decamped, and Sherman was able to lead his men on a leisurely march back to Chattanooga. The gateway to the heart of the Confederacy had been flung open by the defeat of Chattanooga.

Left: *Union General George Thomas, the "Rock of Chickamauga," charges Orchard Knob, capturing it in a single day and providing Grant with an excellent command post from which to oversee the entire field of battle at Chattanooga.*

Right: *With his men from the Army of the Potomac General "Fighting Joe" Hooker stormed up the rugged slopes of Lookout Mountain, overcoming Confederate forces and hoisting the U.S. flag at the top. Here Union army officers pose on top of Lookout Mountain.*

Left: *On the right flank of the battlefield at Chattanooga, Missionary Ridge rose 200 feet above the plain and was heavily defended by Confederate troops from its foot to the crest. The zealous Army of the Cumberland, without orders to do so, surged to the top under a hail of musket fire, routing the defenders.*

Commander of the Armies

Grant sent for Julia to join him in Nashville, where he established his headquarters to wait out the winter. There, at the beginning of March 1864, he received orders to report to Washington immediately. He was not unaware that an unprecedented honor was awaiting him – his Galena congressman friend, Elihu Washburne, had indicated as much. That honor was the commission of lieutenant general in the Army of the United States, a rank hitherto held in full only by George Washington.

On March 8 Grant arrived in the capital modestly, without fanfare, his 14-year-old son Fred his sole companion. Through a mixup no one met their train. At the Willard Hotel he registered simply as "U.S. Grant and son, Galena, Ill." There was nothing about his appearance to impress the clerk or an onlooker with his military distinction. Of medium height and spare frame (5′ 8″ weighing 135 pounds), he wore a rumpled, tarnished officer's coat over slumped shoulders, walked with a loping and not at all military gait, and spoke in a quiet, almost diffident voice. No regalia, no retinue, no air of authority or command, unless you happened to notice his square-set jaw beneath the short, light-brown beard.

It was not long, of course, before Washington was buzzing with the news that "he" had arrived, the hero of the North, whose popularity outmatched that of the President himself. Later in the day he learned that he was expected at the White House that evening when the Lincolns held one of their regular Tuesday receptions. He walked the two blocks to the White House, alone, leaving Fred behind, and stepped into a hall more crowded than usual, for the word had got around he might be present. From across the room Lincoln recognized him and came forward to shake his hand, welcoming him warmly. At last the two men from Illinois, the mentor and the captain, met, the President towering some eight inches above his guest. Grant pulled shyly at his lapel as the President started to talk. Then their eyes met, the clear blue eyes of the general and the brown eyes of Lincoln with their underlying shadow of sadness, and each recognized in the other that faith in their common purpose and dedication to its outcome that bonded them.

The following afternoon Grant formally received his commission in a ceremony at the White House. Henceforth he was subordinate to no one but his and the nation's Commander-in-Chief. Halleck was given a new title as chief of staff, which meant he would continue to concern himself with administrative chores and deal with the intrigue and divisive political pressures that prevailed in Washington.

A desk in the capital had no appeal for Grant, his place was in the field. He left for his new headquarters at Brandy Station, Va., 50 miles distant, close to Culpeper, to join Maj. Gen. George Meade and his Army of the Potomac. Seven years Grant's senior, his victory at Gettysburg overshadowed by his failure to pursue Lee's army in its retreat, Meade offered to relinquish his command to Sherman or another general from the army in the West, an offer Grant graciously rejected. He had other plans for Sherman, whom he at once put in command of the western armies, with orders to go down the Western and Atlantic Railroad toward Atlanta, take that city, and move on from there to his prime objective, Joseph Johnston's Confederate forces, in control of most of the territory between the Gulf and Virginia. The plan was for total destruction, not only in attacks on fighting men but of everything in sight, the land and its ability to sustain the life of its people. Gen. Franz Sigel, with 26,000 men spread over Maryland and West Virginia, was given the task of driving through the Shenandoah Valley to deprive Lee of food and support from that quarter. Another army under Grant's command, headed by the controversial Brig. Gen. Benjamin Butler, on Virginia's Peninsula between the York and James rivers, was to advance to City Point, just south of Petersburg, its ultimate goal the taking of Richmond.

Grant actually made few changes at the top of the army's

After Chattanooga Grant established headquarters in Nashville, Tennessee, with his troops. Seen here is the camp of the 125th Regiment of Illinois Volunteer Infantry.

command. One man he brought from the West was the feisty, bantam-size son of Irish immigrants, Philip Henry Sheridan, among those who had charged up Missionary Ridge and chosen now to head a new Cavalry Corps of the Army of the Potomac. Before the year ended Sheridan would have written his name in history. Ambrose Everett Burnside, another general who had aided at Chattanooga by taking and capturing Nashville, was placed in command of a corps of the Army of the Potomac. He too was to play a principal role in the forthcoming campaign, without writing his name in history.

As Grant prepared for his direct confrontation with the one opponent he held in awe, Robert E. Lee, he had every reason to feel he held the edge. With the North's significantly greater population, he had the advantage of calling on a far larger number of men to serve in the ranks of the Union army than available to the manpower-depleted South. Altogether, as the campaign got under way at the beginning of May, Grant had some 120,000 men in active service. Always better supplied and provisioned by the industrialized North and with the full backing and resources of the Federal Government, the Army of the Potomac that spring of 1864 was in top condition compared with its war-worn, impoverished, ill-equipped adversary.

At best Lee could count on no more than a force of 62,000 for the campaign about to be launched. But these men were acquainted with every inch of the difficult terrain that was to be the battleground, with its thick woods, thickets, brambles, meandering streams, the heat of the day, the sudden rains that turned everything into a quagmire, not to mention their acquired immunity to malaria. There was also the fact that *their* land was being invaded. And then there was the quality of the leadership, of Lee himself and his generals. Lee had already defied the odds, as well as the conventional rules of warfare, and was possessed of the native genius that in the military art, as in the practice of any art, is refined by both victory and defeat. Despite the loss of some of his best generals, above all, the incomparable Stonewall Jackson, he could summon a proven team - Richard S. Ewell, J. E. B. Stuart, Fitzhugh Lee (his nephew), Ambrose Powell Hill, Fighting Dick Anderson, P. G. T. Beauregard, James Longstreet, Jubal Early, all men he had fought with and could count on for their best.

When Grant chose to cross the Rapidan River at midnight on May 3 and attack in the area called the Wilderness, he was reasonably confident that he would take Lee off guard and cut him off from Richmond, perhaps even capture his whole army in one swift battle. He had not reckoned on the cunning of Lee's scouts, and Lee's ability to move his army up quickly and force the enemy to fight while still groping its way to a position where the kind of fighting it was trained for was feasible.

The Battle of the Wilderness was a harrowing nightmare for both sides. Disoriented in the thickets, hopelessly entangled in brambles and undergrowth, the men often grappling at almost point-blank range or shooting at an enemy dimly visible only by the flashing of guns, the desperate contest swayed back and forth two days and nights. During the second night forest fires set off by gunfire raged, and the entrenched armies listened through the impenetrable darkness to the screams of the wounded and dying trapped in the flames.

At a pivotal point during the fighting Lee, riding his beloved horse Traveller, abandoned his usual dignified

Top: *French artist Louis Mercier made this etching of Le Général Grant soon after the Civil War. European countries followed the conflict with much interest and sometimes sent observers to the scenes of battle for an on-site look.*

Above: *Philip Henry Sheridan rose quickly in the Union army from unpromising lieutenant to general and head of cavalry. His ravaging forces and fiercely aggressive tactics hastened Lee's surrender at Appomattox.*

composure when the Texas Brigade under Brig. Gen. John Gregg thundered past the wreckage of Hill's corps. Waving his hat, he shouted, "Hurrah for Texas! Go and drive out these people." (He always referred to his opponents as "these people," never the enemy.) Then, with reckless enthusiasm, he began riding forward with the Texans and was only reluctantly persuaded back by Longstreet, who told him with masterly understatement that it would be better to ride to some place of safety "as it is not quite comfortable where we are."

The dawn of May 7 found the Federal soldiers huddled in their entrenchments, the smoldering forest around them, rain falling steadily. They assumed, when Grant and Meade were seen conversing privately by the roadside, that they would shortly be ordered back across the Rapidan to regroup and replan. Grant was standing thoughtfully, cigar in mouth, slowly whittling away at a stick he held in his hand, a common practice of his. Suddenly he turned, and the order

they were awaiting was given. But it was to move south, not north. They were to advance that night to Spotsylvania Court House. Grant's decision was based on his calculation that the Army of Northern Virginia was headed for Richmond. His aim was a left flank movement to cut them off. His calculation proved wrong. Lee had foreseen exactly what he was up to and had Stuart's cavalry in place to meet the Federal cavalry led by Gouverneur Warren at 8 o'clock the morning of May 8 at the crossroads of Spotsylvania. The opposing armies would fight to a standoff for the next seven days. On May 12 the Federals broke the Southern line at a spot known to history as the "Bloody Angle," a horseshoe-shaped salient of breastworks. There Grant lost one of his finest corps commanders, Gen. John Sedgwick, picked off by a Southern sharpshooter a moment after boasting "They couldn't hit an elephant at this distance." No bitterer fighting than that of Spotsylvania ever took place on the American continent. By the time it drew to a close Federal

Right: *The telegraph was extensively used by both sides during the Civil War, the Federal Government creating its own military telegraph system. Grant is seen here writing news of the crossing of the Rapidan River, May 3, 1864, to be wired to Washington.*

Opposite page: *Moving south after Spotsylvania, Grant and Meade made a stop at noon on May 21 at Massaponex Church, Virginia, for an informal council of war with their staff, seated on pews brought from the church into the tree-shaded yard. Grant is leaning over pew at left studying a map for routes.*

casualties were 17,500 out of 110,000 engaged, making a total of 33,000 losses since the Wilderness Campaign began. Though the South's losses are uncertain, there is no doubt that slowly but methodically Lee's manpower and capability to wage offensive war were eroding.

Meantime Grant had sent Sheridan off on a raid around the Confederate lines. Jeb Stuart, the 31-year-old flower of the Confederate cavalry, got wind of it and pursued Sheridan to forestall his reaching Richmond. At Yellow Tavern just north of Richmond the morning of May 11 Stuart was ready for Sheridan's cavalry when it arrived at noon. During the ensuing attack he was mortally wounded while firing from his horse. Shortly before, he had said to a fellow officer that he did not wish to live in a defeated South. The following day he died in Richmond. The Age of Chivalry in battle was over. The future of the war would belong to the hard, the grim, the ruthless as epitomized by Sheridan, for whom war was synonymous with devastation.

On the morning of May 21 Grant and Meade started moving southward. After going about three and a half miles they made a predesigned halt at Massaponax Church, on the main north-south artery connecting Fredericksburg and Richmond, where temporary headquarters were established. Pews from the Baptist Church were moved into the yard beneath two shade trees and a sort of council of war was held to discuss, among other things, the routes Burnside was to take that night after the withdrawal from Spotsylvania. A photographer traveling with the headquarters column, Timothy O'Sullivan, set up his gear and produced a set of memorable glimpses of that interlude. From the seemingly leisurely scene of Grant, Meade, Charles Dana, John A. Rawlins, with their staff officers and their horses in the background, it would be difficult to guess that an hour later they would be on the move again in their deadly mission to get between the Army of Northern Virginia and Richmond.

For once the weather favored them with dry roads as they neared the North Anna River, a placid stream with high banks luxuriantly wooded with oak and tulip trees. Confident they were making a surprise attack, the first Federal troops crossed the stream on May 23. Lee was waiting, strong earthworks in place and his forces firmly entrenced astride the main routes to Richmond. Despite a series of attempts Grant was unable to find a vulnerable point in the Confederate defenses. All that came of the "surprise attack" was a day of skirmishing.

Lee's failure to attack led Grant to conclude that the Army of Northern Virginia was fast fading, its men clinging to their safety behind their entrenchments because they were not up to battle in the open. Feeling now assured, he swung his forces around to Lee's right, only to find Lee awaiting him at Topotomoy Creek. Still persuaded that success over his canny, but certainly weakened, foe was only a matter of time, he headed for Cold Harbor about 10 miles east of Richmond. It was to be an assault he would always regret, as he acknowledged in his *Memoirs*.

Cold Harbor was neither a harbor nor was it cold. It was a dusty crossroads important to both armies, consisting of nothing but a tumbledown tavern in a triangular grove of trees. The temperature throughout those early days in June hovered close to 100 degrees. It provided ready access to reinforcements that Federal transports had brought down the James River and up the York to the Pamunkey River slightly to the East.

Fitzhugh Lee's cavalry division was on the outskirts of Cold Harbor when in the early afternoon of May 31 pickets warned that Sheridan's troopers were coming. By late afternoon the Confederates had abandoned their defenses, and "Little Phil" took the crossroads. That night Sheridan's cavalrymen threw up temporary breastworks while a sizable Federal corps made a grueling march to come to his support. By the morning of June 1 Cold Harbor was in

Right: *A Union army corps throwing up a double line of breastworks the night of May 6, 1864, in the Wilderness as Grant launches his final contest against Lee in Virginia.*

Below: *Though the Federals broke the southern line at Spotsylvania, no bitterer fighting ever took place. A major loss to Grant was that of one of his finest commanders, John Sedgwick.*

Grant's hands. He ordered an attack for dawn on June 2, postponed for a day because the first contingents made a wrong turn in the dark, took a long way around, and were in no condition when they did get there by 6:30 AM for more than sporadic skirmishing. By late afternoon rain had set in so heavily that any offensive operations ended for the day. By the next day, June 3, Lee had gained the time his veterans needed to dig a network of trenches with artillery skillfully placed to fire on every avenue of approach.

From them on everything went wrong for the incoming Federal troops. Overconfident, no one from Grant's or Meade's headquarters reconnoitered the Confederate posi-

tions. Corps commanders were given no specific instructions, but left to decide on their own where to hit Confederate lines and how to coordinate their actions. As one angry corps commander, William Smith, said to his staff, there was "an absence of any military plan," the whole attack was "simply an order to slaughter my best troops." And that was exactly what happened day after day. In less than an hour some 6000 men were destroyed and the survivors hopelessly pinned down. Even the Confederates called Cold Harbor "Grant's slaughter pen."

Strangely, Grant and Meade continued not to grasp what was happening. Either could have enlightened himself by inspecting the field of battle. Instead, attack after attack was ordered. The moans of the wounded and dying went unheeded because medical teams could not get to them. Throughout the army, criticism of the offensive was strongly voiced. By June 7 Grant and his staff finally faced up to the bitter reality that direct-offensive tactics to overwhelm Lee would not work. Grant had lost five men to Lee's one, a total of 50,000 since he crossed the Rapidan. His officer corps was severely decimated. There was nothing left but to withdraw from the attempt to get at Richmond from the East.

Though Lee had adroitly held off direct thrusts at Richmond, he had been unable to drive the Army of the Potomac back to the North. His losses had been also heavy, and he could not hope for the influx of fresh men and supplies that Grant could call on. Though Lee's tactics had so far succeeded, Grant held the strategic advantage. Lee could not move now without exposing Richmond.

From the disastrous frontal assaults at Spotsylvania and Cold Harbor, Grant had learned that a new way had to be found if he was to outsmart Lee. He pulled all his troops back in a grand loop and down toward the James River out of sight of the keen-eyed Confederate pickets on the Chickahominy River. His object was to sneak up under Richmond to its back door, Petersburg, 23 miles south of the Confederate capital. To achieve that he had to get the immense army across the James River quickly before it could be observed. Ferries alone would not do the whole job. With skillful preplanning and expert engineering a 2100-foot pontoon bridge, the longest, strongest, and most flexible ever built, was thrown up in half a day across a chosen spot in the river and the men quietly moved in a vast maneuver between June 14 and 16. For the first time Lee had lost Grant completely and left Petersburg in the command of Beauregard with only 2200 men to hold its fortifications. William F.

"Baldy" Smith and his Federal corps of 16,000 borrowed from Butler's Army of the James was sent ahead to make a lightning swift attack on the morning of June 15. Grant was so convinced of success that he wried Halleck he would have Petersburg secured before Confederate reinforcements could arrive. Indeed, Charles Dana, who was traveling with Grant, also wired Washington that "All goes on like a miracle."

The miracle did not take place. Smith was slow in acting, he did not attack until dusk. Meanwhile, a supplementary force under Winfield Scott Hancock, whom Grant had ordered that morning to hurry to Smith's aid, was delayed by a combination of avoidable blunders – faulty maps, hazy orders, and an unnecessary stop for rations. And when Hancock did arrive, Smith did nothing with his men but have them occupy the few trenches they had captured. The night was frittered away by lack of adequate and coordinated direction all the way down the line from Grant and Butler to the timid and hesitant Smith.

By next day Beauregard had alerted Lee for reinforcements and shortened his lines until Lee's army began arriving. By June 18 a major Union attack was repulsed so vigorously that in just 30 minutes one regiment lost 632 of its 900 men, the highest casualties of any Union regiment in a single battle during the war. Four days of storming the Petersburg entrenchments cost the North a total of 11,386 killed, wounded, and captured out of 63,797 engaged. The opportunity of taking Petersburg when it was weak had

Union troops crouch in a captured trench and exchange fire with Confederate soldiers barely yards away in a horseshoe-shaped salient of breastworks known as the "Bloody Angle" during battle at Spotsylvania Court House on May 12.

been lost. Only one course was now left to Grant – siege. It was to be a long one, nine and a half months, through the miserable summer and all of fall and winter until the end of the following March when spring came again to Virginia.

Since early in the war the North had been organizing black regiments as one solution to the problem of slaves who had becom refugees, either as fugitives or because of Union victory in territory that had belonged to their owners. Race prejudice in the North was widespread despite the anti-slavery position of the President, and in the beginning these "colored regiments" as they were designated were rather disdainfully entrusted only with garrison duty or

even given the hard menial work white soldiers considered beneath them. Little by little, however, a sort of adjustment took place, especially when the realization dawned that a black soldier could stop a Rebel bullet as well as a white soldier. Eventually 150,000 blacks were organized into well-trained regiments, always under a white commander who was a volunteer seeking thereby to obtain an officer's commission. Except for their commanders, these troops were not integrated, they were made up only of black soldiers.

This differentiation explains a decision by Grant in the dramatic "crater" explosion of the Petersburg siege at the end of July. A lieutenant colonel commanding the 48th

Left: *Taking on his foe at a dusty crossroads 10 miles east of Richmond called Cold Harbor was an assault Grant later admitted he would always regret.*

Below: *A lack of specific instructions combined with inadequate coordination of Federal troops and actions resulted in such wholesale death and destruction at Cold Harbor that men on both sides referred to it as "Grant's slaughter pen."*

Grant at his camp headquarters a mile and three quarters northeast of the Cold Harbor crossroads, which he occupied until the afternoon of June 12, 1864. He was then 42 years old and rapidly approaching the height of his fame.

Pennsylvania Regiment, Henry Pleasants, a mining engineer by profession, got the idea of digging a tunnel just 130 yards from where his men were entrenched, filling it with powder, and blowing up the Confederate fortifications directly above it. The idea was passed along to Burnside, who agreed, to Meade, who thought it claptrap, to Grant, who said go ahead, recalling a similar technique he had used at Vicksburg. Work on the tunnel took about a month. When ready, four tons of black powder were placed in eight magazines and the explosion timed for very early the morning of July 30. Burnside had planned to have a division of black troops under Gen. Edward Ferrero, especially trained for the occasion, go in first to spearhead the assault after the explosion. Grant put a stop to that, figuring prudently that if the whole thing should prove a failure, it could be said they were risking the lives of their black soldiers because they did not care about them. So it was the white division of Gen. James Ledlie (chosen by drawing lots) who went into the crater after the spectacular eruption that tossed earth, men, guns, carriages into the air, creating a 500-yard, 30-foot deep gap.

That gap was a cluttered chaos of tangled wire, bodies and broken guns, carriages, timber, and other debris, en-closed by precipitous walls some 80 feet high. The black infantry were now sent in, but, with no chance of using the invasion techniques in which they had been drilled, were cut down. The leaderless men were scrambling for a way through or up or out when a Confederate charge led by Brig. Gen. William Mahone rushed up from above and rained mortar shells upon them from every direction. The butchery was appalling. No one had had the foresight of providing ladders for the trapped men to make their escape. Neither Burnside, Ferrero, nor Ledlie was on hand with troops to help them. Ledlie and Ferrero were passed out dead drunk in a bombproof at a safe distance. The whole operation, which had started with the explosion at 4:45 AM, was over shortly before 1:00 PM. Federal casualties were some 4400 out of 20,708 engaged; Confederate, about 1500 of 11,466. Ledlie was subsequently cashiered in disgrace, Burnside allowed to retire gracefully, and the hapless Ferrero transferred to some innocuous post elsewhere.

Grant settled in at City Point, Virginia, a small town on the south side of the James River that provided an excellent landing site for an immense supply depot. Wharves lined the shore, and food and matériel of every sort poured in like a flood from transports and barges. Grant chose a two-

room planked cabin for his headquarters in preference to the grand manor house in the compound, which he turned over the use of his quartermaster-general, Rufus Ingalls, his plebe-year roommate at West Point. From there he directed operations fought over a 1000-mile sweep of a vast segment of the continent. Several rooms had to be added to the cabin as Julia and the children regularly visited him there. As did, among other emissaries, the President.

If ever Lincoln needed his chosen general, he needed him that summer of 1864. In the upcoming November presidential elections it appeared, as things stood, that he would be defeated. The North had never been wholly united on the war, and Lincoln's administration was being increasingly blamed for failure to end hostilities and restore harmony. If Lincoln were defeated for the presidency, Grant would go down too, and with them their common goal of the survival of the Union.

With new and hardened resolve Grant quickly set in motion a series of operations as carefully calculated as they were unheard of in the tradition of warmaking. On August 1 he put the ardent young Sheridan in command of all troops in the Shenandoah Valley with instructions to follow the enemy "to the death." Nothing and no one was to be spared. Farms were to be destroyed, crops and livestock carried off, all males treated as prisoners of war whatever their military status, and all Negroes removed to prevent further planting. He rejected Lincoln's plea for the suppression of incendiaryism. "If the war is to last another year we want the Shenandoah Valley to remain a barren waste," he told Sheridan. The families of John Mosby's cavalry force, adept at guerrilla attacks, were to be rounded up as hostages and the raiders themselves, when caught, hanged on the spot without trial. Furthermore, he informed Secretary of War Stanton, he had ordered a stop to exchanging prisoners in camps on either side, knowing full well that since the Confederates had not enough food for their own fighting men, there would be none for their prisoners.

The Army of the Potomac was to keep Lee's army bottled up in Petersburg so none could be detached and sent south to aid Johnston's forces contending with Sherman's advance to Atlanta. The capture by Adm. David Farragut on August 5 of the southern port of Mobile Bay, Ala., closed another Confederate gateway to the outside world. An event remembered today for Farragut's battle cry as he bulled his ships through a Confederate mine field, "Damn the torpedoes – full speed ahead!"

As Sherman edged ever nearer Atlanta, Jefferson Davis made one of his many mistakes in judgment. In July he removed Joseph E. Johnston from command of the Army of Tennessee, replacing him with Gen. John Bell Hood, thus rendering Sherman, as he later wrote, "most valuable service." Hood was a pugnacious and brave fighter – he had lost his left arm at Gettysburg, his right leg at Chickamauga, and led his men against Sherman strapped to his saddle. But he was no master of command. Not that the depleted Confederate forces had any real chance against the three armies of 110,000 men Sherman led. The story of the taking and burning of Atlanta on September 2 is today a romanticized legend, if no less devastating by being a film spectacle. Its impact on the re-election of Abraham Lincoln, and the fate of Grant himself, was critical to the course of American history. Doubts about "Lincoln's war" were removed by Sherman's occupation of Atlanta.

In eastern Virginia, Jubal Early's dauntless Confederates continued to harass Sheridan's ravaging forces. In mid-October Sheridan was returning from a brief visit to Washington when Early launched a surprise attack on the Union camp in Cedar Creek, dislodging two corps and seizing prisoners and arms. Sheridan had just arrived at Winchester 20 miles away when he awoke the morning of October 19 to the sound of distant gunfire. He was off and away on horseback toward Cedar Creek in a flash, galloping with all the dash glamorized in Thomas Buchanan Read's poem *Sheridan's Ride*. Rallying his men, he drove off Early's outnumbered attackers. It was the last battle in the Shenandoah Valley. Sheridan had carried out the dread mission Grant had given him. He had turned the beautiful, fertile valley Stonewall Jackson had fought so masterfully to preserve at the beginning of the war into the "barren waste" Grant had ordered. Commissioned a major general, Sheridan joined Grant to continue wearing down the Army of Northern Virginia besieged at Petersburg by cutting railroads and

Opposite top: *Members of the U.S. 107th Colored Infantry Regiment on duty outside the camp's guardhouse. Some 300,000 black troops served in the Union army.*

Opposite bottom: *Petersburg, Virginia, a rail center, was the focus of Grant's attack the summer of 1864.*

Right: *On July 30 Federal forces blew a huge crater from a tunnel they dug under the line defending Petersburg, inflicting heavier casualties on their own men than on the enemy.*

canals and destroying southern supply depots. Pleased by his combativeness, Grant enlarged Sheridan's corps to three divisions and assigned the cavalry the status of an independent army in the impending campaign. With the proud ferocity he still cherished when he wrote of it years later, Sheridan desired "my cavalry to be in at the death." It was.

In Georgia, Sherman left Atlanta on his famous – some would say infamous – march to the sea, arriving in time for a December 21 message of holiday joy to Lincoln: "I beg to present you, as a Xmas gift, the city of Savannah." The postholiday message he delivered to the people of South Carolina as he pushed northward after the first of the year held no joy, only revenge in full as the price of their being the first state to secede. His men evened the score with Charleston for firing on Fort Sumter four years earlier by systematically

Having gained control of the James River, the Union army was able with the help of pontoon bridges they constructed to land stores of supplies for their forces fighting in Virginia.

vandalizing, despoiling and wrecking its beautiful homes. The state's capital, Columbia, fared even worse. In a single night two-thirds of the city was reduced to smoldering ashes from wind-fanned flames set off by fires for which Sherman disclaimed responsibility, but whose instigation no one in Columbia doubted.

At his headquarters in City Point, Grant was gracious host on February 1, 1865 to three unusual guests, commissioners from Richmond, one of them the Confederacy's vice president, Alexander Stephens, bringing feelers for a negotiated peace. They spent an amicable evening over dinner, Grant getting on particularly well with Stephens. Mindful, however, that he had not the authority to dabble in political affairs, he sent a careful message to Washington. He did not attend the conference of Lincoln and his Secretary of State William Seward with the three commissioners on the Federal vessel *River Queen* in Hampton Roads February 2. A "negotiated peace" was, to Lincoln, unthinkable. Until the Confederate armies were disbanded, the national authority accepted by all the states and slavery abolished throughout the South there would be no peace.

Left: *From 1864 to the end of the war Grant had his headquarters at City Point, Virginia, on the south side of the James River, with wharves lining the shore and a military railroad to handle a continual inflow of cargo, and with accommodations for his staff officers as well as for visiting emissaries, including President Lincoln.*

Left: *Union entrenchments before Petersburg during the long months of its siege. Muddy and confining, they were a breeding ground for disease.*

Left: *This 12-inch caliber mortar, dubbed "Dictator," stands ready to be fired on the fortifications at Petersburg by the Union gunners grouped behind it.*

Spring Campaign 1865: Road to Appomattox

And so the war dragged miserably on. Except for Petersburg, Grant's fronts were now secure. Sherman was heading toward North Carolina with an army of 100,000 to deal with Johnston's pitiful force of 20,000. In the trans-Mississippi Thomas had halted the last threat of a major Confederate offensive, having soundly defeated Hood outside Nashville in December.

The one anxiety haunting Grant as he approached his second spring in Virginia was that somehow Lee would slip out of his grasp, move his small army into the hills and prolong the war another year by guerrilla fighting. He had to break Lee's lines at Petersburg and close all possible means and routes to his escape.

Lee had been forced to extend his lines to their utmost limits until in February 1865 he was entrenched from north of Richmond to south of Petersburg. Initial Federal attempts to break those lines were inconclusive. But, finally, a Con-

federate full-scale attack March 24 on Fort Stedman, a Federal stronghold serving as a supply line to City Point, ended in a costly Confederate defeat. The Union forces had handled with ease Lee's last, best effort to break their hold on Petersburg.

By chance, Lincoln was visiting City Point at the time. He was attending a scheduled divisional review with Grant the afternoon of March 25 as the fighting was winding down. A Confederate prisoner being led off while the review was under way marveled to see the President and Grant riding by on horseback as if nothing had happened. All the Southerners present agreed then "with one accord . . . that our cause was lost."

After months of deadlock at Petersburg the spring campaign of 1865 moved with breathtaking suddenness. On Sunday, March 26, Lee informed Jefferson Davis that he could no longer hold his position and would have to get the

Right: *Grant with Sherman and Sheridan, the two generals he relied on most the final year of the war. A deadly trio, they carried out a new military concept – Total War.*

Opposite page: *Union troops crossing the Pamunkey River at Hanover Ferry, Virginia, over a hastily laid but sturdy bridge erected by the army's expert engineers.*

Right: *Union General Francis Barlow in front of Confederate earthworks 12 miles from Richmond, whose impending fall precipitated the flight of Jefferson Davis and his cabinet and Lee's withdrawal of his troops from Petersburg.*

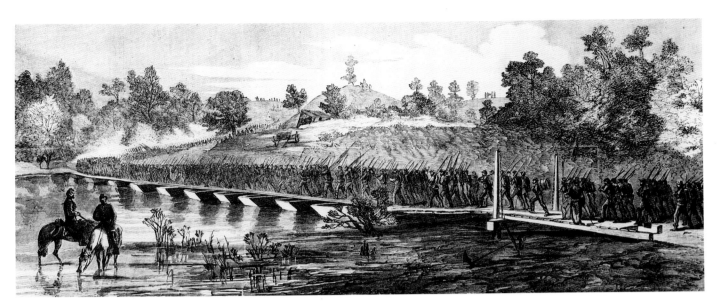

army away and try to join up with Johnston to continue the fighting elsewhere. For more than a month Grant had been expecting Lee to attempt a juncture with Johnston, and had planned a massive movement to prevent it. His field of operations would spread out in a rectangle southwest of Petersburg. The western side of that rectangle was a road leading north to the Southside Railroad by a crossroads called Five Forks. There the last real battle of the war was fought. On March 31 and April 1 Phil Sheridan's troopers, supported by infantry, took on a division under George Pickett (of the heroic, if disastrous, "Pickett's Charge" at Gettysburg) and Fitzhugh Lee's cavalry sent by Lee to block Federal movements. Pickett was driven back to Five Forks by the wildly dashing, threatening, swearing, fist-shaking antics of Sheridan. Of the fewer than 10,000 men the Confederates had to fight with 5000 were captured.

Grant immediately ordered a general assault on the main Petersburg lines at dawn Sunday, April 2. In the futile defense of Fort Gregg another of Lee's most valued and faithful lieutenants, A. P. Hill, was slain.

Jefferson Davis was in his pew at St. Paul's Episcopal Church in Richmond that morning when a message from Lee was slipped to him that the Confederate capital would have to be evacuated immediately. Davis, with members of his cabinet, quietly boarded a special train that evening for Danville, Virginia. Before evacuating Richmond, Confederate soldiers were ordered to destroy factories, arsenals, warehouses and mills to prevent their falling into the hands of Federal occupiers. By the next day whole sections of the city were gutted by flames and ravaged by looting mobs of drunken deserters and riffraff. On April 4, with Federal forces now in control, Lincoln traveled up the James River from City Point to tour the stricken city.

Lee started westward on his last march with what was left of the Army of Northern Virginia. His immediate objective was Amelia Court House on the Richmond and Danville Railroad. There he hoped to pull together his varied units, traveling by five separate routes, and distribute the large stock of provisions he had ordered sent there as he was leaving Petersburg. His foot-weary, hungry men were buoyed as they trudged on behind him by the prospect of the good meal awaiting them. But not a pound of food for the hungry men or a bale of hay for the horses had arrived at Amelia Court House. Instead of turning south, as he had intended, to join Johnston in North Carolina, Lee had to continue west, rounding up what food he could from farmers and foraging and eluding Grant, who had hurled his mighty armies in pursuit the moment he learned Lee was on the move. Grant sent Sheridan's swift cavalry ahead to block Lee's line of march until the infantry could bring the Confederates to battle. Severe clashes at Sayler's Creek and Farmville April 6 and 7 reduced the weakened Confederate forces still further. Still Lee, joined now by Longstreet, pressed west, ever in the hope of reaching his supplies, which he learned had been sent to Lynchburg, and outrunning his pursuers.

Grant reached Farmville April 7 just after Lee had left. Sitting on the porch in late afternoon, he addressed a letter to the Confederate general, saying briefly: "The results of the last week must convince you of the hopelessness of further resistance on the part of the Army of Northern Virginia in this struggle. I feel that it is so, and regard it as my duty to shift from myself the responsibility of any further effusion of blood, by asking of you the surrender of that portion of the C.S. army known as the Army of Northern Virginia." He sent the letter off to Lee by flag of truce. Receiving it several hours later Lee passed it to Longstreet, whose response was quick: "Not yet." Remembering Grant's reputation of Unconditional Surrender, Lee was wary. His reply was careful. His situation was not so hopeless, he said, but he too wished to stop the bloodshed and wanted to know what terms were being offered should he consider surrender.

That night his column moved steadily onward into the bright dawn of April 8, headed for Appomattox Station, 22 miles west of Farmville, where the supplies he was expecting had been forwarded from Lynchburg.

The day wore on with further exchanges between the two generals, Lee hedging on the exact terms of surrender, still half-planning for a breakthrough westward beyond the Union lines. For Grant that day of waiting and wondering was, quite literally, agony. He was beset by one of the sick headaches that occasionally afflicted him and that no remedy could relieve. In the farmhouse he shared with Meade and their staffs he was kept awake half the night by the piano-pounding of one of the officers. Music was at the best of times discordant to his ears.

With no final word from Lee by Sunday morning, April 9, Grant mounted his horse Cincinnati and, despite his still throbbing head, went on a long ride around his army. The best thing that could happen to him that day, he told his aide Horace Porter, would be for the pain of the headache to clear. That "best thing" did happen, somewhat after noon. A courier sent out nearly two hours earlier finally located him. The message was a request from Lee to discuss "the surren-

der of this army." Grant smiled. Suddenly his headache was gone, he felt wonderful. He sent Orville E. Babcock of his staff ahead to say he was on his way.

Sheridan had learned of the supplies at Appomattox Station and gotten there first, trapping Lee at Appomattox Court House three miles from the station. With Federal cavalry on one side and infantry on the other, Confederate attempts at attack had proved useless.

Lee was awaiting Grant in the parlor of the home of Wilmer McLean in Appomattox Court House, chatting with Babcock. A patriotic Southerner, McLean had moved to this sleepy little community from Manassas after the first major battle of the war had been fought over his land. His was the most prosperous-looking residence in the village, a two-storey brick structure with a colonnaded porch. Use of it had been at the persuasion of Col. Charles Marshall of Lee's staff.

Lee rose to his feet as Grant entered the room, followed by members of his staff and Generals Ord and Sheridan. For Grant the long, hard-fought pursuit was finally over. Yet as the two men shook hands an unknowing observer from afar might have been confused as to which was the victor and

which the defeated. Lee, tall, erect, dignified, was impeccable in his handsome general's uniform with his finest sword in an English scabbard at his side. Grant, shorter by four inches, slouched, mud-spattered from his ride, his plain sack coat unbuttoned, wore no accoutrements of his rank except his three-starred shoulder straps on an ordinary soldier's uniform. Certainly nothing in his rather awkward, almost embarrassed, manner hinted of the glory of victory. It was Lee who, when Grant, in an effort to be polite, talked on at some length about the old days in the army in Mexico, brought him back to the main point by saying: "I suppose, General Grant, that the topic of our present meeting is fully understood. I asked to see you to ascertain upon what terms you would receive the surrender of my army."

Opposite page: *The ruins of an arsenal in Richmond, Virginia. Before evacuating, Confederate soldiers were ordered to burn factories and military depots to prevent Federal occupiers from seizing them.*

Above: *This burned out street was but one of many such sites Lincoln found when he visited the stricken city on April 4.*

Overleaf: *Federal soldiers in front of the Court House at Appomattox, April 9, 1865, where the Army of Northern Virginia was finally trapped by Sheridan's forces and Lee had no choice but to accept Grant's request for surrender.*

Right: *Routes and positions of the opposing armies in the Federal advance on Richmond.*

Inset below: *The military career of Ulysses S. Grant, a West Point graduate, had come to an end until the Civil War proved his exceptional ability for leadership and action and won him the highest post in the land, general in chief of the U.S. Army.*

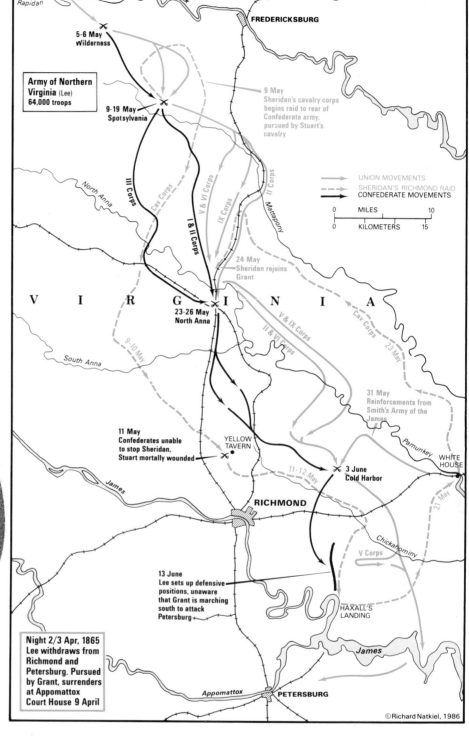

Army of the Potomac (Meade) 99,000 troops
Overall Union command: Grant

+IX Corps (Burnside) 19,000 troops

2400 hrs, 3 May 1864 Grant begins advance south

MARYLAND

Potomac

Germanna Ford

Rapidan

Rappahannock

FREDERICKSBURG

5-6 May Wilderness

Army of Northern Virginia (Lee) 64,000 troops

9-19 May Spotsylvania

9 May Sheridan's cavalry corps begins raid to rear of Confederate army, pursued by Stuart's cavalry

North Anna

III Corps

Cav Corps

V & VI Corps

IX Corps

II Corps

Mattapony

UNION MOVEMENTS
SHERIDAN'S RICHMOND RAID
CONFEDERATE MOVEMENTS

0   MILES   10
0   KILOMETERS   15

I & II Corps

24 May Sheridan rejoins Grant

V I R G I N I A

23-26 May North Anna

V & IX Corps

Cav Corps

23 May

9-10 May

South Anna

11 & VI Corps

31 May Reinforcements from Smith's Army of the James

Pamunkey

WHITE HOUSE

11 May Confederates unable to stop Sheridan, Stuart mortally wounded

YELLOW TAVERN

11-12 May

3 June Cold Harbor

27 May

James

RICHMOND

Chickahominy

V Corps

13 June Lee sets up defensive positions, unaware that Grant is marching south to attack Petersburg

HAXALL'S LANDING

James

Night 2/3 Apr, 1865 Lee withdraws from Richmond and Petersburg. Pursued by Grant, surrenders at Appomattox Court House 9 April

Appomattox

PETERSBURG

©Richard Natkiel, 1986

At Lee's suggestion Grant wrote out the terms himself, in pencil, with the same clarity and directness as so many times he had written out orders for his men. The terms were fair and generous: the officers and men to be paroled and disqualified from taking up arms until properly exchanged, and all arms, ammunition and supplies were to be delivered up as captured property. The officers could keep their sidearms, their private horses or baggage, return to their homes not to be disturbed by U.S. authority so long as they observed their paroles and the laws in force where each resided. When it was all written out, copies made and signed by each general, Lee hesitantly put forward one last request. Explaining that the cavalrymen and artillerists in the Confederate army owned their own horses, it would be a favor if they too were allowed to keep them. Grant keenly understood, from his own earlier life, the need of those horses in getting a crop started back on the small farms to which the men would return destitute and with families to support. He willingly assented, though it was not in the terms as written.

As they were parting Lee mentioned that his men had been long without food, and he had none to give them. Determining from Sheridan that 25,000 men could be supplied, Grant asked Lee if that would do. It would. (Ironically, the supplies Sheridan had intercepted at Appomattox Station were more than sufficient to meet the need.)

It was a little after 3:00 PM when it was over. As Lee emerged from the McLean house the Federal soldiers in the yard came to attention and saluted. When his horse Traveller was brought, he reached up and smoothed its forelock, then climbed into the saddle. Coming down the steps of the porch just then, Grant stopped and removed his hat. Lee raised his hat in return, and then rode slowly off into the waning afternoon toward the heartbroken men who had served him with such loyalty. There would be for him that Palm Sunday no hosannas.

The exultant Federal camps erupted with joy and began to fire salutes. Grant silenced them. "The war is over," he said. "The Rebels are our countrymen again."

The message Grant sent to Washington at 4:30 PM was brief, without emotion: "General Lee surrendered the Army of Northern Virginia this afternoon on terms proposed by myself. The accompanying additional correspondence will show the conditions fully."

It would have done Lee little good if he had managed to break through and join Johnston, whom Sherman was already holding at bay in North Carolina. With fewer than half the men of the Union army, not all of them fully armed and organized, Johnston would have been driven to surrender soon even without the news from Virginia. On April 18 these two generals, each known as the other's most pitiless enemy, signed an astonishing agreement of peace, in which Sherman went far beyond the limited military terms of the document Grant drew up and promised general amnesty for all Southerners and a pledge that the Federal government would recognize all the state legislatures of the South as soon as their officials took an oath of allegiance. He was severely criticized in Washington, and the generous political provisions of the agreement were annulled.

Below: *Scene of the surrender of General Robert E. Lee and his army to General Grant in the McLean House at Appomattox, Virginia, April 9, 1865.*

Left: *On the eve of the capture of Richmond civilians and soldiers escape in rapid flight over a bridge in the foreground to a backdrop of flames from fires raging through the evacuated city.*

A Political Career

By Friday, April 14, Grant was in the capital with Julia. Lincoln invited them both to join him and Mrs. Lincoln at the theater that evening. Julia had been subjected at City Point to the demeaning conduct of Mary Lincoln toward other wives, and enough was enough. After conferring with her privately, Grant excused them on the grounds they were taking an afternoon train to Burlington, New Jersey, to join their children, who were in school there. And so Grant was not in the box at Ford's Theater that evening when John Wilkes Booth fired a bullet into the brain of Abraham Lincoln. It was said, though never proved, that Grant, Vice President Johnson, and Secretary of State Seward were on the list of those to be assassinated that night. Seward, recuperating from a carriage accident, was attacked that night in his home by an assailant, who slashed him with a knife. The only other man in Lincoln's box at the theater, Maj. Henry Rathbone, was stabbed before Booth leaped on to the stage.

Grant returned to Washington the next day, and the Vice President, Andrew Johnson, was sworn in as President. On the train the previous evening, after receiving the news that Lincoln had been shot and would not live, Julia had asked, "This will make Andy Johnson President, will it not?" "Yes," her husband replied, "and . . . I dread the change."

He had met Andrew Johnson once before, at Nashville, when he had set out for Chattanooga for the decisive battle there. Johnson was then the Federal military governor of Tennessee, and had welcomed him with a long speech. It

had given him a chance to size up the man who was to be an ally and adversary on his own route to the White House.

At the last meeting with his cabinet on April 14, a meeting Grant had attended as an invited guest, Lincoln said: "I think it providential that this great rebellion is crushed just as Congress has adjourned and there are none of the disturbing elements of that body to hinder and embarrass us. If we are wise and discreet we shall reanimate the states and get their governments in successful operation, with order prevailing and the Union re-established before Congress comes together in December. . . . We must extinguish our resentments if we expect harmony and union."

Lincoln knew that the Radicals in Congress would oppose his policy of magnanimity toward the conquered states. And that is what they did, bringing about the dark period known as "the tragic era." Andrew Johnson was no match for the Radical majority in Congress led by the vehement Charles Sumner, Senator from Massachusetts, and Thaddeus Stephens, Representative from Pennsylvania. He was no match, either, for Secretary of War, Edwin M. Stanton, one of the most extreme of the Radicals.

Grant, as army general-in-chief with headquarters in Washington, found himself in the thick of politics. In 1866 he was named full general, a rank not used since 1799. As such he was in charge of enforcing the Reconstruction acts, passed over Johnson's veto, which placed the southern states under military control. Soon he was drawn into the camp of the Radicals in their battle with Johnson. Still

believing Grant was on his side, Johnson appointed him to replace Stanton as secretary of war in April 1867 in defiance of the Tenure of Office Act requiring the consent of the Senate in the dismissal of a cabinet officer. Though at first he declined, Grant assumed the post *ad interim*, but five months later turned it back to Stanton when the Senate refused to sanction the dismissal. This brought on an altercation with Johnson, who accused him of not keeping his word to stay on until he had time to appoint some other man or test the constitutionality of the Tenure of Office Act in the courts. Grant never forgave him for questioning his veracity. Impeachment proceedings against Johnson failed in the Senate by one vote.

In the minds of the Radicals Grant had become the inevitable nominee of the Republican party for the presidency in 1868. It was an easy victory for the hero who embodied to the public the valiant struggle to maintain the Union. He did nothing to seek the nomination and was at his desk at army headquarters when the news of it came. His brief acceptance speech of the Republican party's nomination as candidate, made to a small delegation at his home in Washington, concluded with the all too prophetic statement: "I shall have no policy of my own to interfere against the will of the people." The "will of the people" was a euphemism for the will of the Radical majority in Congress. With Julia he went to Galena, Ill., to wait out the campaign, leaving the speechmaking to his supporters. His chief contribution to the oratory of the campaign was four words: "Let us have peace."

His elevation to the presidency was, according to the biographer W. E. Woodward, as well as to such prominent publications as the *New York Herald* and *Nation* in their obituaries after his death, the greatest disaster of his life. He held the office for two terms, and himself viewed the entire period as one of splendid triumph. It was, in fact, a national disgrace. John Bigelow, distinguished author and diplomat, wrote of Grant soon after the inauguration, "He seems to have no comprehension of the nature of political forces." And during the Stanton affair in 1867, Secretary of the Navy Gideon Welles, recorded in his *Diary* after a conversation with Grant, "It pained me to see how little he understood of the fundamental principles and structure of our government, and of the Constitution itself."

The list of his appointments to the Cabinet was undisclosed until after the inauguration and was a curious hodgepodge, a few of the names unknown to members of the Senate and for that matter barely known to Grant. The senators unanimously accepted the list out of deference to Grant and despite his failure to advise them first. The choice of John A. Rawlins as secretary of war was, of course, without question. He had long been Grant's close and wise friend, conscience of his personal life and a successful intermediary between him and his associates in public duty. In the few months left to him – for he was dying of tuberculosis – Rawlins proved equally effective as the President's moral mentor in the public realm. A man little known to Grant at the time became secretary of state. He was Hamilton Fish, an able, refined, cultivated member of an old New York family, who served the full eight years of Grant's presidency with astute insight and a genuine understanding of his role. Some of the appointments were marginal, and the Cabinet was eventually reorganized with numerous turnovers along the way. The punitive Reconstruction acts adopted by Congress, which in their long-term effects were as harmful to the South's black population they were intended to benefit as to its white, against whom they were targeted, Grant did

Left: *Amid cheering throngs the nation's capital holds a grand review on May 23, 1865, with the victorious Army of the Potomac parading down Pennsylvania and all flags flying full mast for the first time in four years.*

Right: *On April 21 the casket bearing the body of the nation's slain President, Abraham Lincoln, was taken from the Capitol rotunda and put on board a special funeral train for burial in Springfield, Illinois, where today both his home and grave are a shrine.*

The funeral cortege of President Lincoln passes City Hall in New York on April 25 as a grieving public pays its last respects.

nothing to amend. The Radical Republicans were convinced they had done a good job, and Grant went along. Their plan, he thought, must be a wise one, since it was conceived in Congress, which included not less than 50 lawyers, who must understand what was right and just!

A detailed account of the bitter partisan politics and monumental corruption of those eight years would astonish even today's shock-proof public. A phenomenon in American life in that era was the emergence of a new breed of businessmen, men who rose from near poverty to the acquisition of vast wealth by any and every means, including swindling the government. Together with disreputable politicians and high officials of similar inclinations, their schemes left nothing untouched.

Several reputations were ruined, including that of Vice President Schuyler Colfax, when insider dealing that went on in the Crédit Mobilier affair came to light. The Crédit Mobilier was a corporation set up before Grant's administration to promote the construction of the Union Pacific Railroad using 12 million acres of federal land and $27,000,000 in U.S. bonds. Such was the financial juggling

that the promoters obtained mortgages on the road for the U.S. bonds and the land grants and in the end the Union Pacific began its existence flat broke and the government held only a worthless second mortgage. Despite proof that Colfax had received a share of the ill-gotten profits, Grant was convinced of his innocence and wrote him a sympathetic letter expressing full satisfaction with his integrity.

Loyalty to his friends and aides blinded Grant to the possibility of their greed and venality. Such was the case of Gen. W. W. Belknap, appointed secretary of war after Rawlins's death for no better reason than that he had marched to the sea with Sherman. When a House committee exposed extortions by Belknap in selling post traderships in the Indian Territory, Grant forestalled impeachment and punishment, accepting his resignation (thus preventing impeachment) with the explanation that he did not comprehend the reason for it. His private secretary, Orville E. Babcock, seems to have dabbled in various fraudulent schemes. He was put on trial in St. Louis for full-scale bribery in the Whisky Ring, which collected from distillers for letting them sell large quantities of liquor without the Treasury's tax stamp on the barrels. Grant insisted on testifying in his defense, declaring him to be guiltless, the only President ever to have testified in a criminal proceeding instituted by the government. It achieved Babcock's acquittal, and he returned to the White House and his old desk. Grant was soon advised by Hamilton Fish that it was not such a good idea to keep him there, so he found a job for his secretary and former aide as inspector of lighthouses.

The world of business was to Grant a mystery, one that fascinated him. Having himself failed so dismally in his early business undertakings, if such they may be called, he respected those men who had made fortunes by their own efforts. That they were unscrupulous mountebanks he was unable, by his very nature, to imagine. He had only admiration for their superior entrepreneurial abilities. He enjoyed the warmth of the hospitality these moguls extended him and Julia. He was especially flattered by the lavish attentions of those master scoundrels, Jay Gould and Jim Fisk. The good will thus engendered came close to his aiding them, unwittingly, in their plan to corner the gold market.

In the summer of 1869 gold sold at $135 an ounce, with $15 million in gold coins in circulation. Though the country was not on the gold standard, gold was essential to banks, shipping combines, and brokerages in the payment of debts. If the price of gold doubled, it would drive down the value of greenbacks and with it stocks purchased on margin, and weaken currency held by banking and other financial institutions. To guard against such a catastrophe, the President was authorized to sell off government gold reserves to stabilize the price. When Gould and Fisk failed to elicit a response from Grant that their buying up gold was in the best interests of the country, they enlisted the collusion of his brother-in-law, Abel Rathbone Corbin. It was easy enough for Corbin to persuade Grant to appoint Gen. Daniel Butterfield head of the New York sub-Treasury, whose duty it was to warn the government of a precipitate rise in gold, and who was, of course, in on the game. Corbin waited until Grant was off on a visit to Pennsylvania and distant from a telegraph office to signal Fisk and Gould the coast was clear. On September 23 they began buying gold. The prices soared from $135 to $161 before noon. Butterfield sent no warning. The next day, September 24, is known as Wall Street's "Black Friday." Banks defaulted, commodities for export could not be sold, imports could not be unloaded, credit ceased. Getting wind of the crisis, Grant quickly telegraphed Secretary of the Treasury George Boutwell to sell government gold reserves. That put a stop to the scheme and ended the panic. The perpetrators got off scot-free, a congressional committee finding there was no law against cornering gold or pressuring a President. Eventually the government went on the gold standard and an Inflation Bill curbed the issuance of paper money.

That Grant was innocent of any complicity or profit from the corruption that went on during his administration is undisputed. He was simply not aware of it, as he was not aware of what was going on in his cabinet meetings. He lacked the gift of dramatizing his own genuine personal honesty.

His administration was not without its achievements. Among them was establishing the principle of international arbitration through the Treaty of Washington in the adjudication with Great Britain over territorial disputes in the Northwest and in the settlement of indemnities for Britain's breach of neutrality during the Civil War by building Confederate cruisers in English shipyards and manning them chiefly with English sailors. He did much to obtain a humane policy for the American Indian, not easy to do in the hostile climate of public opinion after Sitting Bull ambushed Gen. George Custer at the Little Bighorn. The financial affairs of the national government were put on a sound basis, with taxes reduced, money stabilized, and a

Above: *Ulysses S. Grant as the 18th President of the United States. Elected in 1868, he served two terms.*

Below: *Though a Democrat and critic of Lincoln, Edwin M. Stanton supported him as his Secretary of War.*

law for the resumption of specie payments passed. Much-needed civil service reforms were effected. Above all, perhaps, he succeeded in bringing the country through the factional hazards that followed the near-impeachment of a President. In his last annual message, December 1876, he said humbly: "It was my fortune, or misfortune, to be called to the office of Chief Executive, without any previous political training. . . . Under such circumstances it is but reasonable to suppose that errors of judgment must have occurred. . . . Failures have been errors of judgment, not of intent."

Through the eight years he spent in the White House, he and Julia were happier than they had ever been. It was truly their home, the only home that had ever been theirs that long. They enjoyed their children and family life, the host of relatives who visited often, the honors bestowed upon them. The saddest part was giving up that haven.

Grant left the presidency with only the money he had put aside from his salary and no forthcoming income. He had had to resign from the army in order to be president, thus cutting himself off from a military pension. At that time presidents were dropped from the federal payroll when they left office and received no pension.

He had always enjoyed travel, and now, free to do so and with enough saved for travel expenses, he set out as a private citizen with Julia and his youngest son Jesse in May 1877 for England. He arrived on the other side of the Atlantic as a world figure, cheered by kings and working men as the embodiment of the American ideal, a hero in war and peace. In England the Grants dined with Queen Victoria, in Belgium King Leopold called on him at his hotel informally, in Rome he was received by the Pope. In Athens the Greeks lit the Parthenon for him at night. He visited the pyramids in Egypt and passed through the gates of Jerusalem to the sound of trumpets. Turkey, India, China, Japan – he was feted everywhere and showered with honors. Of the many great men he met and with whom he conversed at length the four who impressed him most were Lord Beaconsfield (Benjamin Disraeli), Prince Otto von Bismarck of Prussia, with whom he shared one of the most revelatory and remarkable tête-à-têtes ever recorded, Léon Gambetta, the French premier, and Gen. Li Hung Chang, the most powerful person in the Celestial Empire, who greeted him with the words, "You and I, General Grant, are the greatest men in the world." The prolongation of the journey to two years around the world was made possible by a modest mining investment that turned out well and substantial profits his lawyer son Buck (Ulysses S. Jr.) in New York had made with his father's money on advice from a new acquaintance, Ferdinand Ward, "the young Napoleon of Wall Street."

Upon his return home in a blaze of glory he was disappointed and chagrined when his name was presented at the 1880 Republican Convention for a third term as President, with 304 votes on the first ballot, ahead of the other candidates. In the end the nomination went to James A. Garfield. "My friends have not been honest with me," he said. "I can't afford to be defeated." It was quite literally true. He had to do something to earn a living.

About this time friends in New York, at the initiative of George W. Jones, proprietor of the *New York Times*, raised a fund of $250,000 by popular subscription for the general and his family. The principal was invested under the direction of trustees, with the income of it going to Grant. He gave up the residence in Galena, moved to New York, and settled into a solid brick house at 3 East 66th Street.

He had grown rather corpulent with age, walked with a limp from neuralgia; his chief pleasures the company of his wife, children and grandchildren, his ever-present cigar, and the continued adulation of the public. Yet the old hankering for a success in business had not left him. The opportunity came when his son Buck, married to the daughter of the well-to-do Jerome Chaffee, organized a banking and brokerage firm with that upcoming financial wizard, Ferdinand Ward. He proposed that his father invest in it and become a member of the firm, a factor that helped the business prosper because of the distinction of his name. Ward was all show, a magnificently convincing show for a good while, and no substance. By May 1884 the firm was a staggering failure. Grant had been swindled and left holding the bag. Meantime, the railroad stocks in which the subscription fund were invested ceased to bear interest; the trustees had to inform its beneficiary there was no more money to be had. At 62 Grant was bankrupt and in debt, with insufficient cash on hand for daily household necessities, and no perceivable assets. He had given all his swords and trophies, as well as property he and Julia owned, to William H. Vander-

Above: *First inauguration of Grant as President, March 4, 1869. From the outset his administration was marked by bitter partisan politics, the corruptive practices of politicians, and his own naivete about processes of government.*

Right: *Grant and his cabinet. Secretary of State Hamilton Fish (seated far left) served both terms with insight and intelligence. John A. Rawlins (seated left, full-face), his wartime aide and adviser, regrettably died of tuberculosis within five months of becoming Secretary of War.*

In the 1872 presidential campaign cartoonists lampooned Grant's person and character unmercifully.

bilt as security for a loan of $150,000 he made in good faith when Ward assured him it was only a matter of tiding over for a day or two. (Vanderbilt forgave the loan and later donated the swords and trophies to the U.S. government, which placed them in the Smithsonian Institution.)

An attempt was made by friends to help him by getting Congress to pass a bill reviving the rank of general he had

given up when he became President, with a provision for his retirement immediately on full pay. The usual partisan politics defeated the bill several times. This refusal to restore to him his honors so hard-won added to his humiliation.

But Grant did have one asset left. The editors of *Century* magazine had been trying for some time to persuade him to write a series of articles on his war experiences, at $500 an article. He had declined, saying he was not a writer and, besides, he had put the Civil War behind him. Now he had no choice. The publication of the first article on the Battle of Shiloh boosted the magazine's circulation enormously, and the fee paid to Grant increased. The proposal was then

THE TIMES DEMAND AN UPRISING OF HONEST CITIZENS TO SWEEP FROM POWER THE MEN WHO PROSTITUTE THE NAME OF AN HONORED PARTY TO SELFISH INTERESTS
B. GRATZ BROWN

advanced of his writing his complete memoirs of the war. The publisher of *Century* thought it might have a sale of possibly 25,000 copies and offered a royalty of 10 percent on each copy sold. That is when another man, who had himself dabbled in business ventures, stepped in – Samuel L. Clemens, better known as Mark Twain. The two men had been friends for some years, and smoked many a cigar together in the house on 66th Street reminiscing about life on the Mississippi. Twain had established a publishing house, Charles L. Webster & Company, to distribute his own books. Getting wind of the project for Grant's *Memoirs*, he saw their value on a far grander scale than the publisher of *Century*. And he was willing to make a far grander offer to obtain the rights for his publishing firm, 20 percent on each copy sold or 70 percent of the profits. Fearing the publisher might stand to lose money on the 20 percent royalty, Grant opted for a share of the profits. It was the one wise "busi-

Top: *The opposition in 1872 had a heyday deriding what they charged to be "Grantism."*

Left: *Julia Dent Grant, whose love and loyalty were ever-sustaining through peace and war, hardships and triumphs.*

Overleaf: *One of the last pictures of the Grant family at Mount McGregor in 1885, outside Saratoga Springs, with Nellie and Fred standing, Jesse far right beside porch rail, Ulysses Jr. seated left on steps, along with daughters-in-law and grandchildren.*

Above: *Grant's catafalque being drawn through the streets of New York to the tomb bearing his name on a high bluff above the Hudson River.*

Right: *Ulysses S. Grant (1822-85) as history remembers him – a general who became great by conquering all odds.*

ness" decision he ever made. Three hundred thousand copies of the *Memoirs* were sold, providing his widow with $450,000 in royalties. The two volumes were regarded then, as still today, as among the great military narratives of history.

Grant was not to live to enjoy the fame or fortune from his book. In the fall of 1884 a sharp stabbing pain in his throat was diagnosed, too late to be operable, as malignant cancer at the root of his tongue. It spread rapidly. He continued writing, first at a desk and, as his strength weakened, on a large pad of paper on his lap. Throughout the winter the disease and the book progressed side by side, the agony of one made endurable by his resolve to complete the other. It had always been his habit to stick to the path on which he had started until he reached the end, whatever the difficulties and detours along the way. He completed the last chapter about a week before he died on July 23, 1885, in a mountaintop cottage at Saratoga Springs, New York, where he had been taken in June for its cleaner and cooler air. Just a few months before his death his army commission as general was restored with retirement pay for life. The news reached him too late to awaken in him a flicker of interest. Among his last visitors at the mountaintop cottage was his old friend from West Point days, Simon Bolivar Buckner, with whom he had ridden into the countryside outside Mexico City, from whom he had borrowed money when he arrived back from the West Coast broke and in disgrace, and of whom he had demanded "unconditional surrender"

in defeating him at Fort Donelson. When asked by reporters about their reunion, Buckner said it was "too sacred to discuss."

The funeral car that bore Grant's body to the vault built for him at Riverside and 122nd Street above the Hudson River in New York was accompanied by a phalanx of generals, comrades along with former foes, members of the executive, legislative, and judicial branches of government, state governors, and foreign dignitaries on his long last march from City Hall past millions of mourning spectators lined up every step of the way. It was as though he was once again coming back to the glory of victory in a hard-fought war, the nation's hero.

Julia Grant lived another 17 years, comfortably, in a house she bought on Massachusetts Avenue in Washington, the city where she and Ulysses had spent their happiest years in another, and grander, house on Pennsylvania Avenue. She was buried beside him beneath the high granite dome known as Grant's Tomb. The tomb, symbolically, faces south, toward Appomattox.

Index